intimate portrait of the world's most successful singer & songwriter

Paul McCartney
Now&then

by Tony Barrow and Robin Bextor | edited by Julian Newby

First published by Hal Leonard Corporation 2004
7777 Bluemound Road
P.O. Box 13819
Milwaukee, WI 53213

Trade Book Division Editorial Offices
151 West 46th Street, 8th Floor
New York, NY 10036

Published in Great Britain by Carlton Books Limited
20 Mortimer Street
London W1T 3JW

Library of Congress Control Number: 2004100968

Printed in the United States of America
First Edition
Book Designed by TK

Visit Hal Leonard online at www.halleonard.com

contents

This is not a biography of Sir Paul McCartney but something far more personal and out of the ordinary.

It is a series of snapshots that together form a picture of the man who it could be argued did more to change the face of popular culture than any other. As the vanguard of the social explosion that came to be neatly termed The 60s, The Beatles during their reign as the greatest show business phenomenon on the planet wiped away years of class differences, rode the wave of mass fame and adoration that helped to create that new post-war age group – the teenager – and, most importantly, dispelled for evermore the myth that being truly creative and artistically viable was in some way the preserve of an academic or elite class. Here was art for everyone, and if you were up for it you too could do your thing, form your own band, and write your own songs.

This book brings to one place a carefully selected series of eyewitness accounts, which the authors exclusively assembled for this project – an array of very real memories that help to form an honest profile of the man they call "Macca". The book's sources include Sir Paul himself, plus a central figure from the tight inner circle of aides and business associates that surrounded him in the 60s when he was part of The Beatles. Our supporting cast includes Sir George Martin, Peter Asher, Donovan, The Rutles' Ron Nasty (Neil Innes), Brian Wilson, Steve Miller, Michael Lindsay-Hogg, Pete Best and the late Bob Wooller.

Robin Bextor

Robin Bextor bought Beatle records when they came in green paper bags and had a hole in the middle. He still has every one and his most treasured possession is a signed copy of *Sgt Pepper*. He is an award-winning film and TV producer and has made programmes on subjects ranging from heart transplants to the British Schindler, which won the Columbus Film Festival top prize. He has also made hundreds of pop videos and full-length films on great British institutions such as Windsor Castle, the Queen Mother, Bad Manners, Mick Jagger, Eric Clapton and UB40. His film company, New Wave, is one of the leading producers of music videos and DVDs. He has filmed many live shows including those of his daughter, Sophie Ellis Bextor, the Queen's Jubilee concert featuring Sir Paul McCartney, Pink Floyd and The Damned, who make him smile more than any other music act. He spent two years writing, researching and editing a worldwide special on Sir Paul in 2001 that actually took a lifetime to produce. During that time he had the opportunity to meet all the major characters from The Beatles' past and present as well as getting a chance to stand on the Apple roof. He has written for many newspapers and magazines, the book to accompany the TV series *Crown And Country* in addition to a number of screenplays and all the end-of-season videos for his beloved Fulham FC. He lives near Richmond in St Margarets – where The Beatles filmed all their movies – with his wife Polly and family. He has three daughters, Sophie, Dulce and Maisy, and a son, Bertie. They all love The Beatles.

Tony Barrow conducts a press conference with the Fab Four.

Tony Barrow

When Brian Epstein wrote to the record columnist on his local newspaper asking if there was any chance of getting a bit of publicity for a group he was signing up called The Beatles, the reply came from someone he'd never heard of, named Tony Barrow, a Liverpool-born writer who was based in London.

Tony had been writing a weekly pop-record review feature each Saturday for *The Liverpool Echo* since 1954 but because he was a schoolboy when the column started, he had been told to make up a nom-de-plume instead of using his own name. Tony called himself Disker and towards the end of 1961 it was Disker to whom Epstein wrote in the hope of getting a write-up on The Beatles.

Epstein eventually went to visit Barrow at his office at the Decca Record Company's London headquarters, where his other job was to write the sleeve notes for the covers of the company's new LP and EP records. It was Decca that soon afterwards famously turned down The Beatles after a disastrous audition.

During the first half of 1962 Epstein made a point of picking Barrow's brains to find out the names of the best record producers in town and the friendliest journalists on the music trade papers. And when he'd done his deal with producer George Martin at EMI, he sought further help from Tony: "At first I hesitated because publicising an EMI band from behind a Decca desk seemed somewhat unethical, but I had the time, and I was already 'moonlighting' by writing my weekly column, so I agreed a fee of £20 with Epstein and set about my first PR assignment for the Fab Four."

The assignments didn't stop for the next six years

Now....

It was one of those nights in New York when it seemed like the whole city was focused on just one person. Every time I flicked through the channels of the TV in my hotel room there he was. It was like a speeded-up version of *Anthology*, one minute he was playing "Hey Jude", the next he was a mop top on the Ed Sullivan show, then he was on the roof of Apple, then meeting the Maharishi, then waving to the audience as he made his way from the stage at Candlestick Park. Images of Paul that were so well known to me and everyone else of my generation that they have become more than pictures of The Beatles. They are the wallpaper of our lives, they shaped the cultural landscape and those images neatly encapsulated an era when real music ruled and for the first time the inventiveness of four ordinary lads seemed boundless and totally without limits.

As I made my way towards the Waldorf, where the Rock & Roll Hall Of Fame was getting ready to induct its most celebrated son, the hubbub was extraordinary. The outside broadcast trucks, satellite dishes, news cars, sparks and catering trucks stretched for blocks around midtown Manhattan. In a land where celebrity is the richest currency of them all they were here to pay homage to the number one. His fame almost defines the term. With The Beatles he was in the most famous act there's been, for God's sake. Now he stands alone at the absolute zenith of the music business – in fact, of all show business – and New York wanted to make sure that he knew just how much they value him.

As I showed a full house of passes and accreditation to the third rank of vetters and checkers, wading through oceans of packed snappers standing six deep behind barriers, the first faces I saw in the foyer were those of two legends, Jimmy Page and Ahmet Ertegun. I made my way through to the green room, which tonight was just a glorified holding area for the world's music elite. There was Neil Young, Bono, Eric Clapton, Bruce Springsteen, Billy Joel, Robbie Robertson, a movie star or two for good measure, and still they were arriving.

In the corner stood Sir George Martin, elegant and virtually immobile in all the chivvying for places, the preening and the posturing. He too was being honoured tonight. He turned to me and quietly said in his distinctive and measured tones, "Just wait to see how this lot react the minute Paul arrives." I didn't know quite what he meant.

Five minutes later I saw it exactly. A huge whisper ran around the room, I hadn't heard anything like it since I was at school and the classroom had been left unattended; when the teacher was on his way the classroom went from activity to silence. And so did the green room. The expectation was enormous, and then through the door waltzed, well, actually, more sort of glided, the object of all our attention. And the entire collection of noble rock stars just froze. The silence was palpable.

Paul McCartney stood just to the side of the doorway, his daughter Stella at his side. He looked slighter than you would imagine, wearing a grey suit and T-shirt; he was talking to Stella, yet his raised-eyebrowed eye somehow scanned the room at the same time.

It was uncanny how the whole room was there to pay deference to this man, just as the awaiting media were. The musicians in the room, big stars, genuinely famous across the planet and rightly full of their own achievement, seemed to unite in recognising that here was the head boy, the role model that defined pop star, that personified creativity, song writing and fame.

Paul seemed to barely acknowledge the effect he had on the gathering; he didn't miss a beat. Just nodded vaguely in my direction and then went into a huddle with George Martin before the huddle became a scrum and the gathering just focused in on him.

That night at the awards he played rock and roll in a scratch band that had all the above and a few others guesting. But Paul was the conductor, the man they took their lead from as he strode through a few rock classics, many of which were written by him. Billy Joel thundered out "Let It Be", Paul swayed along but really took off for "Blue Suede Shoes", "Good Golly Miss Molly", the sort of tunes he had played when a savage young Beatle.

When he took his award from Neil Young and was inducted into the Hall Of Fame he thanked the room and said the award was for Linda. He insisted that Ringo and George, who was ill at the time, should also be honoured. You felt like he was being gracious in taking the award but that really it meant little to him. There is nothing he hasn't won, really. He spoke entirely without nerves and managed to completely reduce the formality of the evening to an informal chat, which made me think that he, unlike practically any other performer I had watched closely, was completely without stage fright. A couple of years later I was at Buckingham Palace as Paul led the Jubilee concert and in front of millions just coolly strummed the *Abbey Road* ditty "Her Majesty". No mean feat, considering.

But then from 40 years ago if you look at a recording of The Beatles' first Ed Sullivan show, he doesn't appear to be the least bit nervous. But he told me he was. Just before they went on – before the curtains opened because it was done like a live theatre show – the floor manager came up to him and said there would be something like 80 million people watching. The most testing time was when Paul, barely 21, came to sing "Yesterday", solo, with a string quartet, but even then he managed to hold it together. The Beatles always did on those big occasions. To this day McCartney still meets American people who tell him how their fathers used to talk about The Beatles' first few television appearances on the Ed Sullivan Show, a couple done in New York and one from Miami Beach, and the Dads always think they wore wigs. The Dads never liked them at the start but they were converted over the years. Everyone was.

McCartney further defied the Hall Of Fame's Oscar night formality by calling his daughter to the podium. Stella wore a T-shirt that bore the legend "About fucking time". As it was completely at odds with American Network TV sensibilities, they tastefully whited-out the offending word. But when Paul returned to the press room, back from the main hall where the awards had been handed out, he insisted on having Stella close by his side throughout. The press, eager to get a picture without the T-shirt, yelled at him to stand away or for her to move out of the way. To English ears they sounded incredibly rude.

Charming, smiling he simply said, "Goodbye fellas" and was gone. I later saw him still in a huddle with George Martin, but pausing every sentence or two to check on Stella, obviously delighted to be out with his daughter. The public part of the evening saw him playing on stage with the band well after the TV recording had finished;

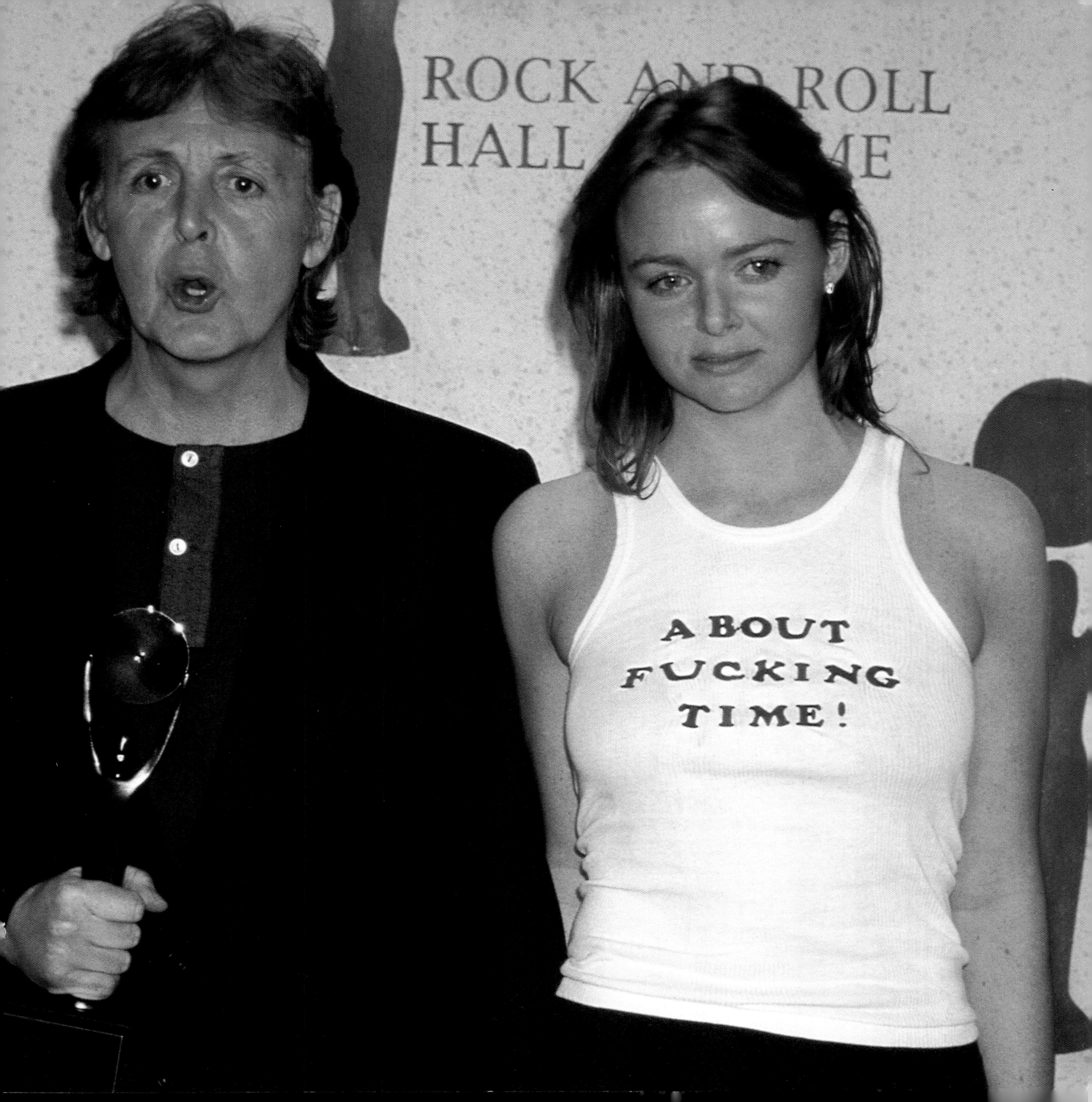
ROCK AND ROLL
HALL
ABOUT FUCKING TIME!

then while most of the gathering was still looking to get a final glimpse of the Beatle, Paul was gone, ever the master at leaving a party.

The evening finished as it had begun for me, walking back through the now quiet streets of Manhattan. On the hotel TV there was still a Beatles fest going on. I supposed it was the same person in the pictures.

About a year later I was driving down the lanes of a small village just outside Rye, past cottages and hedgerows, there was the old pub with its logs burning in the middle of the room, and on top of the windswept hill was a windmill. An unmarked track led the way.

Inside what was formerly the hay barn sat one of the recording machines used at the Abbey Road studio for *Sgt Pepper*. Across the way the main building looks out to Dungeness and the Kent/Sussex coastline. It has a truly spectacular view. All around the rooms and the corridors are photos, beautiful candid prints of Linda's work. In some there are children, in some there are horses, in many is Paul McCartney. Bearded à la "Let It Be", around the time of *Ram*, or in any one of those Wings phases. They reveal a classy, quiet self-confidence that is missing from the publicity photos.

His home is tasteful, considered, the home of an artist. Someone who writes letters in ink, reads a lot, looks at pictures. Hundreds of books, lovely furniture, beautiful pictures on the wall — modern abstract works from the artists you would expect: those that his father-in-law's legal firm represented, like de Kooning and a small Picasso, impressionists, Matisse.

He came into the room in a woollen dark suit, and asked me my opinion. He was lighter than I had last seen him and looking a bit, well, I suppose jaunty is the right word. The words come easy to him. He can talk amusingly and in a self-effacing way. It's a way that doesn't look for praise or judgement but equally doesn't fight shy of clearly being aware of just what has been achieved. He must have met thousands of people from TV, film, newspapers over the years, yet he manages to be utterly charming and has that trick of making you feel special.

I told him I liked the suit, and he was pleased, as it had been a bargain-buy in India. Less than £20, he reckoned. It looked like a very expensive couture suit, and was worn in a casual sense of style that the be-suited likes of Noel Gallagher can only dream about. We then talked about The Beatles and the thing that had changed his life, my life, all of our lives. Opposite sat the man who with three others had sat atop the world. In a class-ridden society they proved that there was a way for talent to win through and in so doing had sparked revolution in hearts and heads.

On the afternoon of Saturday, July 6, 1957, Paul McCartney met John Lennon for the first time in the grounds of St Peters, the parish church of the Liverpool suburb of Woolton village, where John's Quarrymen skiffle group was playing an outdoor gig during a summer garden fete. Paul was persuaded to join John's group and the song-writing partnership of Lennon and McCartney was created. George Harrison got to know Paul as a fellow traveller on the No. 86 Corporation bus, which took them to and from school, the Liverpool Institute, which is now LIPA, the Liverpool Institute of Performing Arts, founded and supported by Paul.

Paul had just turned 15 when he met John who was going on 17. When Paul first saw John he was on stage, he was drinking beers and he

thought he was acting like "a bit of a slob". Paul at 15 was the result of a hard-working Mum and Dad, the strong maternal influence showed itself in his neatness and a desire to be liked. Lennon gave Paul a sense of freedom and rebellion. The young John Lennon took no prisoners. He had been drinking at the fete, he didn't mind acting uncool or showing off with his confident smile. Yet there was clearly something there that impressed Paul.

When he met George, Paul was still 15 and Harrison almost one year younger. Paul has often said how the age difference between himself and Harrison had an effect from the outset – although there was less than eight months between them. It was that inevitable age thing that young boys have, the undeniable desire to establish a pecking order. George got to carry the guitar cases.

But the important thing was that George could play the guitar, better than either John or Paul. He understood the instrument, had even made a crude version of one from a block of wood, one that played best as a slide guitar, Hawaiian style. "My Sweet Lord" had a little bit of slide.

So it was for this reason that Paul recommended him to John, and after an audition on the bus that ran past the end of Forthlin Road, that was it, he was in.

The starting point for McCartney had been the music. Even more than George or John he was aware of the power of music on a social and personal level because his Dad was a musician and regularly played at family parties at his house. The music became exciting when he got hold of a radio and was able to listen to American Forces Radio, Elvis, Little Richard and the rest. But there was something else. Because of his mother's work McCartney lived in a number of houses that

came with the job and became gradually more comfortable as time went by. But early on the McCartney homes were in the poorest parts of Liverpool, and after the war Liverpool was poor.

So part of the dream, undeniably, was to earn your way out of that situation. At that time there were really only two ways to do that for an ordinary working-class Liverpool boy: he could become a footballer or he could join the army. It is absolutely no coincidence that in the 60s it was the baby boom kids, those born after the war in the late 40s and early 50s, who propelled British football back to the top of the heap. The council houses of Anfield, Dagenham in the East End and Glasgow gave rise to teams such as West Ham, who won England's first European trophy in 1965, Celtic who won the European Cup in 1967 and of course the England team who won the World Cup in 1966. Throughout the late 60s and 70s Liverpool, under Bill Shankly, was the standard bearer of British football. By fusing Scots passion and English players such as Tommy Smith, a scouser, youngsters were given a route out of the mean streets of the city by their skill on the football field.

For McCartney sport wasn't the answer and the army was unthinkable. That left music – it was show business after all and McCartney has never forgotten about the money.

He had a reputation for meanness at one stage, but there is no evidence for that; he spreads it around as much as he can, is good to charities and helps youngsters with talent to develop it. When someone has garnered the fantastic financial rewards that Sir Paul McCartney has done, then people are inevitably envious. George Martin once said to me in an unguarded moment that I should imagine for a

The programme for the Woolton church fete where Paul and John first met; the exact spot where the Lennon and McCartney partnership began; Paul's house in Forthlin Road, Liverpool. In a letter to John Lennon written by Paul, and read out by him at Lennon's posthumous induction into the Rock & Roll Hall Of Fame in 1994, he said, "I remember when we first met, at Woolton, at the village fete. It was a beautiful summer day and I walked in there and saw you on stage. And you were singing 'Come Go With Me' by the Dell Vikings, but you didn't know the words so you made them up. 'Come Go With Me to the Penitentiary'. It's not in the lyrics."

moment getting up in the morning determined to spend as much money that day as I could. Buy a car in the morning, walk down Bond Street and stop in every shop and buy more clothes, records, watches, anything, dine in the best restaurants and go to the best clubs and then get home laden down with worldly goods late in the evening to realise that you had earned far more than you spent that day anyway – that is what it is like being McCartney. Finance simply isn't an issue with Paul now.

But in the early days living conditions were pretty tough going. Now it's difficult to understand what the class system was like in Britain at the beginning of the 60s. There were also problems with coming from particular provincial regions. Doors could be shut before they opened.

The Beatles experienced that discrimination later. In Liverpool class largely didn't matter. According to McCartney there wasn't a class system in Liverpool. He remembers that there was only one place which was a bit posh, Mossley Hill. According to him they talked a bit funny up there. It wasn't until they went down south to London that they noticed how everybody sounded like their image of university types. Once he was there, of course, he wasn't cocooned so much among people from his own background. He realised that there were people who talked posh and would talk down to four lads from up North. It became yet another reason to succeed, to show them and everyone like them that The Beatles and in particular Paul McCartney were as good – if not better – than any of them.

It wasn't just social snobbery that The Beatles encountered as they headed the vanguard of youth entering such citadels of the establishment

as the BBC. They felt that there was also a certain amount of snobbery about what music people were listening to.

Once when they were due to record a BBC radio show in London, they came into the studio and found the producers were all listening to some jazz, Oscar Peterson. It was music that Paul was yet to feel comfortable with. The Beatles had hoped that the technicians would be listening to a bit of Elvis so that they could meet on the same musical wavelength whatever their other differences. But the engineers seemed to consider the work they were doing with The Beatles as slumming it a bit, going down a level, and they patronised them.

The changes Paul went through in this period were massive. From the Liverpool of the late 50s and early 60s first he was immersed in a life-changing experience in Hamburg and then had the shock to the system that London gave him. Both left a marked effect. The Hamburg he entered was like Liverpool in some respects. A melting pot, a port, but also it had the added ingredient of the American GIs and they brought with them black music, the genuine versions of the anodised music Paul had heard on the radio.

Somewhere between August and September 1960, between the Casbah in Liverpool and the Indra in Hamburg, the group called themselves briefly The Silver Beetles and then The Silver Beatles before they dropped the Silver and settled for The Beatles as their permanent name. Unfortunately the decision came too late to change the posters outside the Indra club.

On this first of several visits to Hamburg, The Beatles stayed for around four months. If not the group's true birthplace, then the German city's seedy club land was certainly The Beatles' nursery, a hothouse where they worked strenuously through all-night shows in front of rowdy audiences of students, sailors, tourists, pimps and prostitutes. It was not only The Beatles' music that matured and evolved in Germany, it was their entire outlook and image, partly because of their environment but mostly because of the influences of several people they met. One typical Merseyside fan summed up her feelings about the Hamburg effect: "The Beatles went away as relatively naive young boys and came home as fully-fledged men."

It was Germany that forced the Beatles to adopt the familiar four-man line-up. John's original band, The Quarrymen, was really a skiffle group with a variable line-up, which was honed down to John, George and Paul. Original bass player Stuart Sutcliffe left after the Germany experience. They added Pete Best just before they left for Hamburg because part of the contract stipulated they had to take a drummer – the Germans expected them to have one. Then in Hamburg they had to play endless sets, up to eight hours at a time almost every night, and everything about their live performance toughened up. It also meant that they had to build up a bigger repertoire.

But an even greater influence on McCartney's sensibilities came from the liberation he felt from being away from home, coupled with the fact that The Beatles were increasingly adopted by the artistic fringe of Hamburg, the residue of the Beatnik movement. Art school graduates like Klaus Voorman, whose paintings of the period capture the atmosphere so well, his girlfriend Astrid Kirchherr and photographer Jurgen Vollme, made a lasting impression. The influence they had on The Beatles is shown by the fact that almost 40 years

on The Beatles still turned to Klaus, the artist who created the *Revolver* cover, for the graphic work on the *Anthology* series of CDs, books and DVDs.

Paul and John called them the "exis" because they were the so-called existentialists who used to hang out in the same part of Hamburg as The Beatles. They were anti-establishment, outsiders or just art students with attitude. They made an impact on Paul.

The Beatles found themselves in the centre of a creative crowd that welcomed them to try different experiences and ways of looking at life. Stuart – always more interested in the visual arts than the others – became totally immersed in the world of Klaus and Astrid. Paul, while not particularly sad at losing Stuart who opted to stay with Kirchherr when the others returned to Liverpool, also was not slow to realise that these Hamburg students and artists had a cool and a hipness that he had never seen before.

It was a formative time for McCartney on several fronts. Up to that moment the only people The Beatles had mixed with had been on the Liverpool scene. The Beatles had been Liverpool through and through, now they walked the streets of Hamburg in their mock-crocodile shoes with a new sense of confidence and importantly they gained that devil-may-care attitude that won them so many admirers once they hit the big time. They realised they did not have to kow-tow to anyone. It was exactly the same sort of anti-establishment stance that had drawn Paul to Lennon back at the church fete.

The Beatles' initial success in Hamburg gave their self-confidence a hefty boost, making them realise that they were capable of entertaining audiences beyond the cosy environs of Liverpool's so-called Mersey Beat circuit. Foreigners even!

"*Somewhere between August and September 1960, between the Casbah in Liverpool and the Indra in Hamburg, the group called themselves briefly The Silver Beetles and then The Silver Beatles before they dropped the Silver and settled for The Beatles as their permanent name.*"

Over the next several years they would go back for more – playing at the Kaiserkeller (1960), the Top Ten club (1961) and the Star club (1962). They packed them in, they were loud, outrageous, popping pills, staying up all night partying and having sex.

When The Beatles returned home after their German adventures they took Merseyside by storm. The Litherland Town Hall concert soon after their return was seen as the seminal moment when the Cavern's foursome came of age. Recording was the next step. Without Pete, dropped after George Martin's reservations (although he had them about Ringo too), "Love Me Do", "Please Please Me" and "From Me To You" meant the move to London was inevitable.

To begin with the Fab Four were exactly that, a group, and London and its fame were very much a group experience. It was heightened by the adulation they almost instantly achieved in America, where the fans seemed to take to the drummer even more than the other three to begin with. It was what allowed Ringo to become such an important part of the group. As soon as they arrived in London the bonding seemed to be complete. They walked around as a unit, they talked together in a foursome, they could finish each other's sentences and at one point they actually lived together in the same flat, although not for too long because unlike in the fantasy film *Yellow Submarine*, they managed to cramp each other's style.

But collectively they had an impact. Andrew Loog Oldham, The Rolling Stones' manager, remembers them as having group strength and a really strong united image. He had seen them as a four-headed monster, so it led him to design The Stones in a different way, far away from the uniform image and even further away from establishment respectability. But The Stones were from a different background from The Beatles and the Cheltenham of Brian Jones was a long way from Merseyside in every sense. Maybe if it had been left to Lennon they might well have kept their leathers, but they would not have made it on the scale that they did. McCartney's way was to gain acceptance and then play the game on his terms once inside.

It was obvious to the whole world that The Beatles were a group, they looked like a group and they had their own uniform. This uniformity was something for which in later years Paul would be criticised. But he was keen to get The Beatles into the same outfits, because he saw it as a mark of show business attainment. As a child he had been impressed by the sort of look the Red Coats at Butlins or the groups of the 50s had when all in the same outfit. But his style was now more in the mould of pop art fashion that designers like Mary Quant and Pierre Cardin were pioneering. They had nothing of The Shadows or later boy bands about them and, with the exception of George, they always seemed perfectly comfortable in their "uniforms".

The opening chapter of The Beatles' life in London was frenetic and, for once, in accord with their public image. They took the capital by storm and they did it together. If their uniform image worked it wasn't because it was especially calculated, it was simply perpetuated because there was no time or energy left to do anything else. The headlong rush to fame was exhilarating but also dizzying, and every second of the day was used up in making maximum use of their limited PR time. How they found time to write is best illustrated by the comic strip that appeared

"To begin with McCartney says it was very much a group experience, they all arrived in London together and briefly shared the same digs. They walked around as a unit, they talked together in a foursome and at one point they actually lived together in the same flat."

Images from rarely seen
footage of The Beatles, held
in the TSW Archive.

The Beatles meet the media in America.

The Beatles on location for the filming of their second feature film, **Help!**

in *Top Boys*, a fan magazine of the day. In true *Hard Day's Night* style they are pictured writing the next single while travelling together on a train, George showing his individuality by climbing into the luggage rack. It made a change from the previous weeks' strip when they had penned "From Me To You" while in the group van. So perhaps for the last time in their lives they lived and created as one, a hangover from the Hamburg days when eight hours a night on stage helped them to understand – and second-guess – what each other was thinking. While they were working with George Martin in the studio he used to say that between them The Beatles became more than the sum of their four parts.

But they each had their own lives too and in those first few months after the move south the seeds of what became a splintered group were sewn. This was especially true for Paul. As early as April 1963 the potential rift was created, albeit unknowingly, when he met young aspiring actress Jane Asher at a post-BBC-recording party. Living in London immediately set him apart from the other Beatles. While Ringo and John had partners from their Liverpool backgrounds, his relationship with Jane Asher led Paul to the heart of the city's artistic community. It was a direction he embraced full on and the timing could not have been better. London was just about to swing, it was a mecca for new and aspiring actors, designers, artists, and those influences surfaced within The Beatles' work, for example, the movie of *Hard Day's Night* reflected their interests in cinéma vérité. They even contacted the controversial playwright Joe Orton to write the script, much to his excitement at possibly meeting the leather-trousered band, but later they dropped the idea.

It must have been a radical and enormously pleasurable awakening for McCartney to find himself in the hub of the Asher family with Jane taking him to the National Theatre or increasingly to the theatrical fringe that was growing in London. They attended art openings, and Paul became friendly with a pretty hip crowd that was also on the fringes of The Rolling Stones' camp: they consisted of people like art dealer and celebrated socialite Robert Fraser (the man arrested with Mick Jagger at the legendary Redlands drug bust), art expert John Dunbar (who had been married to Marianne Faithfull) and the omnipresent Barry Miles, publisher of *International Times* – who ended up creating The Beatles' spoken word label for Apple. These were erudite, sophisticated people, a world away from the estates of Liverpool, more likely to spend their weekends in Marrakech or at an art gallery opening than on the football terraces at Anfield.

In this company, just as he did during the 90s with the likes of record producer Youth, he was able to use his new friends to gain knowledge of trends and art forms of which he knew little. From Youth he learned about trance music and recorded the little-known *Fireman* album. In the 60s he was able to start his pick-and-mix "borrowing" of influences that led to such glorious pot pourri works as *Sgt Pepper* and the *White Album*.

"I don't want to give the impression that I was the only member of The Beatles who broadened his outlook artistically in London," Paul told me, but equally he admits that increasingly as material success bought the other Beatles huge piles in London's salubrious suburbs, he stuck in the centre of town. From Cavendish Avenue in St John's Wood he would be able to be in Soho in five minutes. London now lay at his feet. No door was closed any more. He was the face to have at

Paul McCartney's London: his home in Cavendish Ave, St John's Wood, a stone's throw from Abbey Road Studios; the orginal Apple Corps Headquarters in Savile Row, Mayfair; the view from the Apple roof where The Beatles played an impromptu concert for the film **Let It Be.**

an opening, or if word got out that he was attending a screening, so would others, keen to get a glimpse.

London somehow seemed much smaller in the 60s. Everyone who can remember tells me so. The Beatles would go around to see The Stones; The Stones would drop in on The Beatles. They'd be on the same bill in television shows or at poll winners' concerts. England's capital city seemed to be Paul McCartney's playground.

Paul dabbled with film, editing his own strange little shorts and then getting Robert Fraser to fix a meeting with director Michelangelo Antonioni, who had made *Blow Up*, so that he could pass comment. When Allen Ginsberg was in town Paul would drop by and think about writing his own poetry, he would hang out with Dylan, play with Steve Miller, go to his Indica bookshop or meet some designers.

It was a freewheeling time and London replaced a university existence for him — except that instead of university digs it was Cavendish Avenue, instead of a bicycle it was an Aston Martin, and his friends and parties were all reported in the national papers.

It was the same sort of cultural path-finding that leed him to the Maharishi, although unlike George who swallowed the entire northern Indian mix, Paul opted for a magpie approach. He took the silence and meditation time to write songs — beautiful songs that grace the *White Album*, like "Blackbird" and "I Will", came during this period — and then he embraced the vegetarian ideals, but Paul also left plenty of the other ideas to one side. "A lot of people went off the guru business. I do agree that many of them were fakes but I don't believe the Maharishi was. To be exposed quite suddenly to something like

meditation was a fruitful thing for us at that particular time in our lives and it's not something I regret for a moment."

Then there were the drugs. Around that time they were naturally meeting people who were into narcotics, first came cannabis. They'd never done it before although the Hamburg experience had been heavily pill-laden, but now the uppers and downers were replaced by reality-changing substances. Paul was never as heavily into drugs as many of his contemporaries and addiction was not a potential risk for him, but it was enough to change his take on everything — and he has always been a supporter of a more lenient legislative attitude to cannabis.

Now every statement he makes on drugs is prefaced by references to how children should be protected and that there are obviously huge perils involved in taking chemicals. But the fact remains that consciousness-expanding drugs played a major part in taking The Beatles, including Paul, onto a different playing field if not into an entirely different game, where the ball was made of candy floss and the other team members had kaleidoscope eyes.

The way the drug experience most obviously manifested itself was in the lyrics of songs — and not just the obvious examples. It also showed itself in their take on what was going on around them and in their relationships. Lennon in particular had huge mood swings.

It showed in other ways too. McCartney allied himself to the anti-war movement, got involved in *International Times*, London's most political of underground newspapers, and started attending radical meetings. What was happening to him on a personal level was happening across the generation. Those fruits of rebellion that seemed so dangerous in those days have resulted in the growth of green politics, equality for gays and women, the animal rights movement and the anti-hunting and anti-fur campaigns. All perfectly reasonable now from today's perspective.

When he was allowed to, either through the cover of *Sgt Pepper* or on the artwork for the *White Album*, these diffuse interests and influences began to surface. A draft for the cover for *Abbey Road,* for example, was drawn out by hand on a sheet of paper for the others to approve, with Paul painstakingly sketching the famous pedestrian crossing with the fabs walking across. When the photographer came to take the photos for the cover he only needed seven goes at it from his stepladder and one was perfect. The irony was that McCartney had actually wanted to call that album *Everest*, a title he felt was in line with their achievements, but getting The Beatles all together for a photo shoot was difficult and to get them all on a plane for the Himalayas would have been almost impossible, so *Everest* became *Abbey Road*.

The *White Album* also benefited from McCartney's contacts and interest in the growing London art scene. Through Robert Fraser, Paul got in touch with artist Richard Hamilton, who at the time was at the forefront of the pop art scene. He then spent the next two weeks visiting Hamilton's home every day, taking over an assembly of photographs from The Beatles' youth, odd snapshots and doodles. Together they assembled a collage in Hamilton's studio on an easel marked up to represent the eventual size of the inlay poster with lines for the size of the album cover. When they found the layout they liked best they then moved on to look at the actual sleeve for the record. With such a thick visual addition as the poster, they thought the minimal all-white cover was the ideal contrast. It was a perfect piece of 60s commercial artwork and had never been attempted before.

Paul then had to guide the concept through EMI's publishing and marketing divisions and also clear the use of simply *The Beatles* as its title. But it was worth the effort; the innovation of that sleeve in taking what was in effect avant-garde elite British fine art into virtually every home in the country should not be underestimated.

The album cover inset also betrayed another aspect of McCartney's increasingly idiosyncratic character. "People must understand one thing about me – I am mad! And I don't mind being mad, it's all right, it's part of my thing. When The Beatles became very famous I missed the anonymity that I'd had as a kid and disguising myself in various mad ways was the answer."

Paul took time out to discover theatrical costumiers, wig makers, disguise experts who could change his appearance, even when he went to New York, for instance. If he got fed up with being a Beatle he could slip into this anonymous looking character with slick back hair, glasses and a big coat. There on the *White Album* poster is Paul's passport photo as that character.

The reaction to the album's poster also clearly shows the media spotlight under which The Beatles did their greatest work. Just one of the many photographs in the collage showed Paul in the bath soaping his hair while lying back in the water. It was a picture that Linda had taken some time before without Paul being aware of it, but immediately on its issue the photo became one of the main planks in the "Paul is dead" rumour. According to some radio commentator the photo proved that Paul had been decapitated. The

"A lot of people went off the guru business. I do agree that many of them were fakes but I don't believe the Maharishi was. To be exposed quite suddenly to something like meditation was a fruitful thing for us at that particular time in our lives and it's not something I regret for a moment."

rumour gathered such pace that at one stage this book's co-author, Tony Barrow, had to go all the way up to the Mull of Kintyre to take a photo of the bemused McCartney to prove to the world he was still alive.

By the mid- to late 60s Paul was the only Beatle with the determination and self-discipline to drive the band's various projects to any kind of conclusion. As the other Beatles withdrew to their country retreats, so Paul's dominance in the studio increased. He became the one with the work ethic and the plans. It might have led to charges of his dominating proceedings. But equally, with John in various stages of medicinal recreation, it was hard to imagine the group continuing with their amazingly prodigious output if McCartney had not grabbed the reins.

Even now he is keen to stress that once all four were in the studio then there was no hierarchy. But that period from 1966 to the end of 1969 is completely unrivalled in terms of quality of output and sheer invention. Abbey Road became a playground for Paul to experiment with these art forms.

The tape loops for "Tomorrow Never Knows" are probably the best example of how Paul's role at this time has been underestimated by a generation of British critics. Derided during his Wings period as being the less creative of the two major songwriting talents in The Beatles, it was Paul who gave the most startling track on Revolver its unique sound. John had originally come up with a great tune that George Martin thought might be best served as a Gregorian-style monks' chant but McCartney saw the opportunity to use a cut-up tape loop system he had been playing around with for some time. Using a makeshift technique of gluing lengths of tape

together and running them through the tape machines at different time intervals, he created a fresh and unique sound. The sounds themselves were from bits of backwards guitar or noises he captured on his travels and then kept in a bag in his greatcoat pocket.

Bemused technicians borrowed tape machines from all the other Abbey Road studios, fed the results through the desk and then mixed them to suit the song just like a modern re-mix. It was that innovative use of the studio as a new extra instrument that kept The Beatles at the cutting edge and that only came about through their decision to stop touring.

The decision to halt the tours had made all the difference to The Beatles' recording work. Paul had been keen to regain control of the music; he felt that the touring had increased their fame but not their creativity. Now they could spend more time writing and more time recording. It was remarkably far-sighted.

"Although we were gaining more and more fame by touring, we were losing our music, losing our souls. During the final tour of America in August 1966, we agreed quietly among ourselves that we wouldn't do any more concerts."

But while moving from being a live band to just a studio band increased the quality of the output it also conversely made their break-up inevitable. The Beatles developed into a launch vehicle for Lennon and McCartney's songwriting talents and George and Ringo became marginalised. For George in particular it must have been incredibly frustrating. Paul's idea of sending out aural postcards to the world via their records rather than appearing in person was great in terms of preserving The Beatles, invincible myth, but it also meant the days of the Star club and those concerts around Britain in 1963 were nothing more than memories and they were no longer the live four-piece that they were.

Filmmaking was another pastime that would replace time on the road, and *Magical Mystery Tour* was a freewheeling attempt at creating the sort of road movie with a series of surreal set-ups that would give them a focus.

The reaction to the film was the first taste The Beatles had of the English press disliking something they had done. In fact the newspapers panned it. Sandwiched between a traditional Christmas television menu of comedy and light entertainment, a freewheeling art-house movie was never going to be too popular.

Those who attended the shoot, like pop star Spencer Davis, confirm that McCartney took the role of director, lining up shots and describing sequences in great detail. Before shooting began Paul had leafed through the actors' directory *Spotlight*, casting the tour bus members for skills other than just acting even if they didn't need to use them particularly.

It was typical of the buoyant confidence that McCartney had at the time that he just took off on the road without a formal script and with a structure so loose it didn't really exist. He got the people from NEMS to acquire a multi-coloured tour bus from the south coast. The actors and The Beatles didn't bother with specific lines of dialogue – just letting it happen, with McCartney sketching out the structure before shooting.

Each evening he would meet in a hotel room with the crew and discuss what they had done, watch any rushes that might have come back, and then map out very loosely what would occur the next day. It was the spirit of Ken Kesey at work. Essentially they made the film up as they went along; even the route of the bus was unplanned, which famously led the coach down a narrow lane where it got trapped on one of rural Devon's smaller bridges.

The "Fool On The Hill" sequence was shot without anyone else, just McCartney and cameraman in the South of France in the hills above St Tropez with Paul looking suitably spaced out and trippy.

The film bears up to fresh viewing now, not least because of the set pieces for "I Am The Walrus" and "Your Mother Should Know", but it also served its purpose in buying The Beatles time and space to get back on track after the untimely death of manager Brian Epstein at the end of August 1967. Through tackling a big project like *Mystery Tour* Paul realised that they could take on other projects, like record making, without the overbearing attitude of a multinational record company. In line with the philosophies behind the editorials of the *International Times* Paul formulated the plan for Apple, a collaborative, co-operative utopian business that promoted talent, and spread the word. All the initial energy came from Paul; weirdly, it was John who seemed most concerned about keeping the role of a manager for the band. Lennon is said to have actually gone for a meeting with Lord Beeching, the minister responsible for closing most of Britain's loss-making train system, for a chat about how to get The Beatles' business back on the rails.

But it was McCartney who came up with Apple. "A is for Apple, this is the start" he told everyone and he took to his role as businessman as he had to film director, with gusto and amateur enthusiasm. Unlike MPL, his publishing company on Soho Square that today purrs with efficiency and has all the hallmarks of a highly successful

"Of all The Beatles he seems to be the one who was hit hardest by the break-up. It was like a divorce and he had not been the willing party, even though he was the one who had to actually draw a line under the group in the High Court."

and thoroughly professional business with office systems firmly in place, Apple bounced along like a wilful puppy, lurching from crisis to crisis. Paul travelled in to work every day, frequently on the bus from St John's Wood, unnoticed in his bearded state. His incisive questioning or innate understanding of business would regularly put some of the more experienced advisers to shame.

But the laissez-faire attitude of the other three – John and George in turns seemed to actively encourage anarchy – combined with prolific drug consumption, meant Apple was doomed to be a glorious and good-natured failure despite one of the most successful releases-to-hits-ratio of any record label and a roster of artists that included Mary Hopkin, Jackie Lomax, Badfinger and James Taylor, while Paul's protégé in A&R, Peter Asher, was at the helm.

As the company unravelled and the excesses became rampant Paul attempted to get his in-laws, the Eastmans, in to save Apple and stop the cash draining out. The lack of money became a frequent subject at board meetings, with private income being used to pay the costs; John even told the press he was down to his last £40,000. With his in-laws Paul came up with a formula to buy the rights to their publishing via the acquisition of Northern Songs (the company formed in 1963 by Brian Epstein, which owned all The Beatles' songs), which undoubtedly with hindsight was the right course of action. But the wrangle went on for weeks and finally the other Beatles – and in particular John, who was championing the services of Allan Klein – made it clear that they simply were not having it. Apple disintegrated and so did the relationships, much to McCartney's disbelief.

Of all The Beatles he seems to be the one who was hit hardest by the break-up. It was like a divorce and he had not been the willing party, even though he was the one who eventually had to draw a line under the group in the High Court. It was more a case of self-preservation in his eyes than breaking up the band.

Even today you can sense that McCartney feels regret at the break-up. Perhaps the fact that he seems increasingly to be taking centre stage as the custodian of The Beatles legacy, he almost has to believe that The Beatles really should have gone on forever. On the other hand perhaps he really does yearn for those days when Lennon was at his side.

Whatever the motivation, he felt that The Beatles had enjoyed some great years and had done some great work and for somebody else to finish up owning it all in the end would have been all wrong.

They were idealistic, and they dreamed, but that wasn't a crime. In fact it was the dreaming and the shooting for the moon that often brought their greatest triumphs. It must be hard for people to enjoy virtually unqualified success in so many ways – from pop stars to musical icons and cultural pathfinders in two great leaps – and then to find that in other areas their feet really are made of clay and that they really are as human as the rest of us. It must have hurt Paul to recognise that they were mortal after all and when he thinks back he finds it hard to believe that they didn't just carry on. But that's an easier position for him to take now; there is no heat in the situation now and the days of battling with Lennon are long gone.

It also ignores the reality of their situation back in 1969 and 1970. The real reason behind the split can be traced back to one of the reasons why Paul was so keen to get The Beatles going in the first place – money. The problem that both John and Paul faced was an increasing tax liability. Paul's lawyers were telling him that if he didn't take action fast there was the real possibility of facing prison for tax evasion. It was unthinkable after everything they had achieved. It was also completely unthinkable to contemplate all that money just slipping away.

Typically, John was more relaxed about his own position. He brushed McCartney off, and clearly antagonised him by meeting McCartney's bristling resolve with a laid-back cynicism. The memos from that time in Savile Row are often vitriolic, frequently totally divisive.

The other factor to consider is that at this time McCartney, in pushing for a judicial settlement, really did not believe deep down that his beloved Beatles would cease to exist. He thought he could push the relationships that little bit harder than anyone else could take. When it became clear that it actually was over, the break-up of The Beatles shattered Paul psychologically. He had work in progress, work he regarded as Beatles work, and now he didn't really know what to do with it. Essentially he was a lost soul.

The band decided to do the photo shoot for their last album – then titled Get Back – in the same place as they'd done their first one and used the same photographer, Angus McBean, to take the pictures in the same location – on the staircase above the foyer in EMI House that they had used on the cover for "Please Please Me".

But The Beatles' Get Back album was never released under that title; it was replaced by Let It Be in May 1970. The freshly shot EMI House images were eventually used in 1973 when EMI released a pair of compilations, The Beatles/

1962–1966 (using the "Please Please Me" shot) and The Beatles/1967–1970, using the Get Back shot. The almost identical poses and the same left-to-right line-up (Ringo, Paul, George, John) provided striking evidence of the visual change in the Fab Four between 1963 and 1969, particularly the length of their four mop tops. It wasn't until nearly 30 years later that Paul was partially able to lay the ghost of those traumatic times with the release of Let It Be ...Naked when he was able to reclaim the songs and mix them like he had always wanted.

"I don't think John wanted to play with his little friends any more but I did, I still wanted to go on playing, so when it was all dashed with the breaking up of Apple, I was the one who was hit the hardest."

All the way through The Beatles' career McCartney would say that they "resembled the four corners of a square". For him it was the right shape and they had the right talent. The times were right too; they were allowed to have access to all the freedom they needed.

At the end, McCartney was hit on a number of fronts. Clearly he had lost, for the time being, his closest friends – the other Beatles. But also he had lost his workmates, the only people with whom he had shared the meteoric rise from Liverpool to world domination. He felt alone, and it might go some way to explaining why he produced those collaborations with Stevie Wonder and Michael Jackson, both artists who like Paul had rocketed to celebrity status while still very young. Unlike John, who was able to take part in Mick's rock & roll circus or jump on a plane to Toronto with Eric Clapton to perform, Paul had a less relaxed attitude to teaming up with other musicians, publicly at least.

interviews

Sheila Johnston, former manager of The Beatles Story, Liverpool

The McCartney name was well known in my house throughout my childhood because my mother, who was a district nurse, worked with Mary McCartney, who was also a district nurse. My mother had taken the post when Mary vacated our house on 72 Weston Avenue, to go to Forthlin Road, which is the house that The National Trust have now taken possession of.

I knew all through my childhood that the McCartneys had moved out of our house. Talking to my mother, she was saying to me "Sheila, there's a letter arrived at the house for Mary McCartney, would you mind taking it down?" We got talking and my mother said that Paul, Mary's son, was in Hamburg at the moment with this band he's got. I put two and two together and it clicked and I said "The Beatles, is he with The Beatles?" and she said, "Oh I don't know what they're called, but they're all playing in a band in Hamburg." That was it, I was on the bus and halfway to Forthlin Road before she'd finished talking. I delivered this letter to Jim McCartney, and Jim, when he knew where I'd come from and who I was, he was very, very hospitable and brought me in. And of course the sad thing was that Mary was no longer there, because she had passed away in 1957. But because this letter had come from the Royal College of Midwives my mother felt that Jim ought to have it, so it was hand-delivered.

We got chatting, Jim and I, about The Beatles and school and music and all those things. He was such a lovely person and he started telling me about this problem he was having with all this fan mail that was coming to the house. He started showing me some of these letters and things that people were writing and we got chatting about it and I offered to help him. I said, "I could help you with this" and he seemed so delighted that someone was willing to share the load a little bit. And so it started there and then. I was invited into the house and we got all this fan mail sorted and out together, and I left the house about an hour later with a huge packet of these letters which I was going to take home and sort out and bring back the next week. But to me it was great, you know, I'd got a reason to go back there. And from there it took off.

One of the most striking things on entering that house was that the front room was full of musical instruments. There was a piano – an upright piano, guitars, a banjo and a trumpet, and I thought immediately, this is interesting, all these musical instruments, and I'm talking to Jim and getting into the conversation more, and I discovered that he himself had been a musician – he'd had his own Jim Mack's Jazz Band throughout the 30s and he'd done the dance hall circuit around the North of England. As we talked more and more, I realised that Jim had actually realised his own musical ambition through Paul, and he was very, very happy and comfortable with what Paul was doing at that time. Although I think that somewhere in the archives of his mind, his intention was to see Paul as a teacher, and Paul had done very well at the Liverpool Institute, he got his qualifications.

But I think Jim was accommodating when it came to the music scene and his musical qualities. But it's a funny thing, Jim McCartney was such a hospitable person, whenever he came to the door you were always invited in and there was always

"I THINK PAUL McCARTNEY AS AN INDIVIDUAL IS REVERED IN LIVERPOOL FOR LOTS AND LOTS OF DIFFERENT REASONS"

a cup of tea and he'd ask, "Have you eaten?". If you hadn't, there was a sandwich and something more than that if you were really hungry. He was always ready to make you feel at home and he was very friendly, but also a very charming and a very gentlemanly person.

He always had his shirt and tie, he always looked very smart, a smart appearance and obviously self-esteem was there. He'd obviously had quite a difficult time since his wife had died with his two teenage boys. I don't mean they were difficult, just the pure practicalities of life, but he'd coped so well and actually had his home the way he liked it and the way he wanted it. So I felt that there was a very disciplined and a very orderly home life there, and the basic qualities and disciplines were in place. I think he'd done a wonderful job on his two boys, as a father in that respect. It's not until much later in The Beatles' story and in Paul McCartney's life that I have actually seen, as Paul got older, those qualities to some degree coming through in Paul, despite all his fame and his fortune.

He seems to have given his own children those same basic standards and quality of life in the way they are and the way they live their lives. I think he's inherited his father's basic respect for life and for other people, which goes a long way. And I can see that, physically, Paul is starting to look a lot more like his Dad. Jim McCartney certainly had that arched eyebrow that is so distinctive of Paul. He was just totally charming and I think Jim, in his own way, dealt with Paul's fame in the same way that Paul has dealt with it himself. It's certainly not gone to his head. He's certainly not become a prima donna, which a lot of people do in his situation. He's just kept his feet on the ground.

I had two elder brothers and a younger sister and when we moved into the house, my father went up into the loft and lying in this box was this little Rupert Bear annual. When I think about it now, it should have really lifted itself out of the box surrounded with a golden glimmer because this little Rupert Bear annual had belonged to Paul McCartney. We just kept it because we loved Rupert. It wasn't until much later when I started to look after The Beatles' fan mail that I took this book down to show Jim and said, "Look, he left this." I was 14 then and Paul must have been about 20 and it was funny because Jim just said to me "Well you can have that, you keep hold of that because Paul's finished with Rupert now", and I took it home, you know, my prize possession. It was one little relic of where our childhood paths had crossed, and I'm very pleased to say it's sitting in a glass case in The Beatles museum in Liverpool now.

I think Paul McCartney as an individual is revered in Liverpool for lots and lots of different reasons. Being a bit of a local historian, see a sort of pattern coming to the surface with Paul's life and he is a benefactor to the city. He'll go down in history with some of the great names, like William Rathbone – people who put so much back into the city, for the public good. What Paul McCartney has done for Liverpool is put into the history books. Because when 200 years from now people read about Paul McCartney, about his work and his life, Liverpool will be the beneficiary of that story because it is about something great that came from the city. The people of Liverpool respect him enormously.

I also think it was very interesting that when Paul received his knighthood he dedicated it to the people of Liverpool.

Pete Best,
former Beatles' drummer

Paul struck me at that time as being very confident, very humorous. And this is before I'd seen him performing. It was just the way he handled himself – he'd do anything for a little bit of a laugh. If there was a laugh going on he wanted to be part of it, it was like, "don't take the attention away from me because I'm still a part of it, anything which is going on I want to be in it".

Humour was a big forte with them in those days, especially John and himself. But it was always, I wouldn't say a battle, but it was interesting for me sitting at the back when they were performing – which goes a little bit away from my first impression of them – but actually to see them play off one another. You know, if John did something and it got the crowd laughing then Paul would automatically respond, you know, to get something, to get the crowd back to him again. And it went on like that but it was, from where I sat, it was great because the crowd was entertained all of the time.

I got a phone call around about August 1960 and it was from Paul. Paul made the initial approach and he said basically, "Pete, we've had the offer to go to Germany, would you be interested? We know you're playing drums and we've seen you playing drums", because I had a little fun band called The Black Jacks – it was just school friends. "And if you're interested then we'd like you to, sort of, you know, do the gig." So I said, "Yeah, it sounds interesting. Let me talk it over with my band", which I did and they turned round and said, "Go for it." And then of course it was clearing it with my parents.

It was like there was this void and they didn't have a drummer and maybe no-one was really concerned about finding another drummer to go to Germany. And Paul being, you know, very much Paul, trying to solve the situation – be in a situation where he's in charge of it, got control of it, maybe he'd taken the horse by the reins and told the others he knew that I played drums and that with their consent he'd approach me.

It was always a two-man show between John and Paul. On some nights Paul would come out on top, and on other nights John would come out on top. What we would do, we would be quite interested to see, like, you know, who was gonna win the cup tonight.

The funny thing was it wasn't something which finished on stage, it wasn't like here we are – six, seven hours a night acting – then, when we came off stage we were different people. It sort of spilled over, it became our lifestyle, you know, our life pattern. The crazy antics would happen on the street, you know, you would have Paul walking up and down the Reeperbahn with a silver toupee on his head, you know, wanting to draw attention to himself. And you'd have John walking down doing the goose step. We were catapulting over one another, rolling, somersaulting on the street. It was like the stage show went on, we'd finished playing the music, but The Beatles were still on show. I think that was why the people of Hamburg took to us.

Paul could wind people up if he wanted to, you know. And there were times when we'd sort of look at one another and turn around and say, you know, "he's just overstepped the mark a little bit" or we'd say, "Cool it down a little bit, like", you know. And I mean Stu was quite a placid person anyway. And we'd seen it happening [the

Pete Best:
" … and the smallest member in the band belted the tallest member in the band, because Paul was the tallest."

"I THINK MY OWN PERSONAL RECOGNITION FOR HIM IS WHAT HE'S GIVEN BACK TO PEOPLE, NOT SO MUCH WHAT HE HAS DONE FOR HIMSELF"

growing rift between McCartney and Sutcliffe], there were a couple of times when, not just myself but John and George, had turned around and said "Look Paul", you know "Leave off it, give him a break, we know what's going on. Just give it a break" like.

Paul continued this particular night at The Top Ten club and as we turned around Stu had put his bass down and the smallest member in the band belted the tallest member in the band, because Paul was the tallest. And we separated them and it was very much a case of like "Back to your corners". But I think that was the only time I'd ever seen anything really volatile happening, you know, between any of the members.

When we came back from Germany the second time, we played Litherland Town Hall. It was a very big gig for us for a number of reasons. It was the first time we'd played on a proper stage instead of platforms and planks and beer crates; there were curtains, the venue was a hall and it was a different kind of audience and a different kind of atmosphere. When we walked into the hall it was different to the clubs we'd played in over in Hamburg, and it was such a different feeling which just made us sort of turn round and look at one another.

It was quite mesmerising. The curtains went back, we were introduced by Bob Wooller, and Bob had fought long and hard to get us this particular gig, it was very much "don't let me down boys, you know I worked my backside off to get you the gig". So we turned round and said, "No we won't do that Bob, just wait and see us." And the curtain went back … and all of a sudden there was just like these screams from girls in the audience. And you could tell from the look on Bob's face as he stood in the wings, it was just

like, "I don't believe this". It was an incredible night to remember. We would have started with "Long Tall Sally" or "Red Sails In The Sunset". Regular numbers which you kicked the show off with. And it would have been Paul. It was nine times out of ten that Paul would open the show.

Paul then suddenly became in his own right, very much a songwriter and an arranger. He would basically turn around and say, "We have the rough bones of it, this is how I see it, this is how I hear it." But he would then leave it up to the rest of the band, so it wasn't a case of, "It's my song, I want this done and this played". It was very much "That's how I think it should go" and then everybody gave input you know, but it came up with a great finished result, which stemmed from him basically, you know. So in later years the Lennon and McCartney songwriting partnership, or McCartney and Lennon, whichever way they deem it, you know, didn't surprise me. I mean the roots were already there. It was just a case of they had their platform and away they went.

He's such a talented guy. It's difficult to say [what his achievements are] because the lad has got so much talent, I mean there's that much pedigree behind him. Where do you start? Is it with the first No.1 he wrote, the fact that he's written a symphony, the fact that he's made a film, the fact that he's been knighted? Well, they are just tips of the iceberg. I think my own personal recognition for him is what he's given back to people, not so much what he's done for himself, and I think that's the Fame school (The Liverpool Academy Of Performing Arts). You can write a concerto and you can write a symphony but that's in a way down to your own talent. But to have to vision, I suppose, to create a Fame school from his own school…

Sir Paul McCartney: "The initial reason for my involvement with LIPA was the building. It was my old school. When I saw for myself the state it had reached as an abandoned building, I wanted to save it."

copper
car

WATER

hard

ethanol

$$CH_3COOC_2H_5 + H_2O \xrightarrow[H^+]{reflux} C$$

Klaus Voorman, part of the Hamburg art school set and, later, album sleeve artist for The Beatles

In the first place the Reeperbahn was somewhere I didn't normally go to. But while walking, suddenly I heard this music in the basement and I thought, "this sounds like live rock & roll to me", so I went in that club and was scared stiff because there were rockers all around. I didn't know what I was getting into – I didn't have any connection with these people. It was Rory Storm and the Hurricanes, I didn't know them but they sounded great and actually Ringo was on drums.

It was interesting because Stuart [Sutcliffe, The Beatles' original bass player] went on stage first and he had those sunglasses on – he looked stunning, just amazing, like James Dean. He walked up on stage and I thought, "He's the boss of the band", he had that aura about him. But he just went up in his corner and plugged his base into his amplifier and the others came on and just got up on stage and didn't say anything, just started playing – I think it was The Hippy Hippy Shake or something like that. It was just an amazing impact.

The first thing was the music, the second thing was the way they acted on stage which was amazing. It's impossible to explain. The thing was, when I first saw them they were jumping up like crazy, laughing, screaming and making jokes in English, which hardly anybody understood. Later on I found out that the boss said, "You don't just stand there – you have to make a show for the

people". That was the trigger for them to do more, and it became ridiculous because they made jokes not just between themselves, but with the audience too. It was a big part of Paul because he was one of those people that interacted, which is a gift that not many people have – to be able to actually talk to people in an audience – and he could do that, and he had a few German words. He and George spoke really well.

We didn't think about our appearance, I at least didn't. I just wanted to see the band and see how they play. Bit by bit I noticed that they were hungry to get something more than they already had – which we admired – and they admired what we were doing [as art students]. From my point of view it was the same thing with Stu, John, Paul and George. It was definitely less of a connection with Pete. Pete was holding back,

and wasn't so interested in us. He always wanted to stay tough and wouldn't let himself off the pedestal, this little shell around him – the others let go.

They played all night, and when they came out of the club there were things happening on the streets, fights and falling over drunks, drugs and prostitution too. And they were just 17 and away

Klaus Voorman:
"They were just 17 and away from home, all living in one of those little rooms, in bunk beds where the water was running down the walls."

Klaus Voorman: "They played all night, and when they came out of the club there were things happening on the streets, fights and falling over drunks, drugs and prostitution too."

from home, all living in one of those little rooms, in bunk beds where the water was running down the walls. They played altogether seven or eight hours a night. They had a really tough time. I think it's the main reason why this band became so strong, because of this long time playing, and building a long repertoire.

When you came to the studios and Abbey Road you could see that The Beatles were thirsty, searching for new things. The aesthetic of doing something tasteful was something they developed from the outset; that isn't something that comes from one person, but several people bouncing off these ideas.

For me [the album cover for *Revolver*] was really hard because I hadn't touched a pencil for years and then John called me and asked if I had an idea for the new album, as yet with no name. He said, "We are in the studio recording it and if you have any ideas you might be able to do the cover". I was thrilled to bits. The things on *Revolver* are still a sensational move forward from all the things they had done before. I was just knocked out by the music. I did about 15 different sketches, ideas. The one with the hair — my favourite, though I didn't say it — was the one they all liked the best. The problem was you had to find a way to express what the songs were in relation to who the buying public are. You couldn't go too far out to crazy artistic things, it had to have valid impact.

Then I went home and did the drawing. I racked my brains, how to do this. Colour didn't come into the picture, it had to be black and white. I'd told them every cover you see is colour, I think a black and white cover is the best. Then I stuck on all the photos, then they saw the finished artwork. Brian Epstein was present with

George Martin and the band. I stood the artwork up and they all liked it very much, Brian even cried, which made me very embarrassed. I got £50 for the cover, and that was the limit. [The record company] said they never paid more than £50 for the cover.

While they were a band they were so strong, the personalities constantly lifting each other up. When they were on their own it was tough — tough for John and also tough for Paul. Each individual is so different that you can't say one coped better than the other, they each had a hard time because they were kind of naked suddenly — and that's human. John and Paul being on stage — of course there's a rivalry going on, but if they'd felt that strongly about it, they wouldn't have been a band. There are lots of bands where somebody would push to get to the front — and that they didn't do. They were very much aware that they were bouncing off one another and that's why they stayed together and made music together. Paul says himself that he wanted the partnership to be called McCartney & Lennon, not Lennon & McCartney — those are the sorts of games that were going on, but they still admired each other so much and they each had their value.

"HE CAN WRITE SONGS QUITE EASILY AND IT WOULD BE MARVELLOUS FOR A MUSICAL TO OPEN ON BROADWAY BY PAUL McCARTNEY"

Bob Wooller, promoter and Cavern club DJ

Paul was a rocker at heart and I often thought that he introduced these softer, gentler, more romantic numbers for his father, who was quite an influence on Paul. Jim McCartney had a dance band way back so he would understand all these songs and no doubt accustomed Paul to them. But one of Paul's favourites which was not one of his own songs was "Til There Was You", from *The Music Man – the Musical*. And he liked doing that. It's a high number. He liked high numbers to show off his voice.

But he wrote all these romantic songs like "And I Love Her", "Yesterday" of course, and my favourite of all his songs, "Here There And Everywhere". What a song that is. You wouldn't credit that a rock & roll musician had done that song. It's so clever of them. Cleverly done, lyrically and musically.

Paul McCartney has an entry in *Who's Who*, and you're allowed to write your own entry. He says words to this effect: "The most significant or important appearance of The Beatles is 27th December 1960 at Litherland Town Hall". So that must have stayed in his mind all those years. Of all the shows they played – they played here at the Cavern nearly 300 times, at Shea Stadium in New York, all over the place, that date is the most important one as far as Paul was concerned.

I always felt that if this group has a leader it is not John Lennon. He may have started the group off, but Paul McCartney was the mainstay of this group.

I used to talk with Paul perhaps more than any of the other Beatles in the back room in between performances. We'd talk about songwriting because I've always been interested in the song – really great songwriters, like Cole Porter, Irving Berlin, Richard Rogers, there's many of them. I used to say to Paul, "You know Cole Porter was a fantastic songwriter, he not only wrote words and music as you do but he has a charm, as you do". Noel Coward was another one. Out of all The Beatles – it's interesting, it was Paul he went to see – basically they came out from some dressing room they were in at some theatre and Coward visited the theatre and he asked if he could see The Beatles and the others stayed in the dressing room. It was probably, well, "bollocks" to Coward, you see. But Paul was very PR-conscious. He went out and saw Coward. And I always felt like that was Paul. He was very PR-conscious and actually he covered to a certain extent some of the outrageous remarks made by John Lennon.

He can write songs quite easily and it would be marvellous for a musical to open up on Broadway by Paul McCartney. I'm not saying he's got to be in it, but songs by Paul McCartney, words and music of course. I think that's something he must get around to.

I think he'll be remembered not because he played the guitar so well and portrayed himself so cleverly, but for the fact that he wrote marvellous songs, songs that would last. On Desert Island Discs in January 82 Paul chose a John Lennon song, "Beautiful Boy". He chose it as his favourite song, so he's not ignoring John Lennon's contribution. But I think if I were to be asked which one do you rate as being the most important, the most significant Beatle of them all? I'd have to say Paul McCartney. And by the way, he said on that programme that he still has the first guitar he was ever given – a Zenith. And he's still got it.

Bob Wooller:
"I used to talk with Paul perhaps more than any of the other Beatles in the back room in between performances. We'd talk about songwriting."

Bob Wooller:
"Paul was a rocker at heart."

"PAUL WILL BE REMEMBERED FOR A VERY LONG TIME BECAUSE HE'LL KEEP CREATING"

Bill Harry, editor of Liverpool music magazine *Mersey Beat*

When we think of John and Paul, people think of the progressive John Lennon and the working-class hero and everything, but in fact it was Paul who had the existence in the council flats, while John had this middle-class upbringing – a nice place in Menlove Avenue, Liverpool, with gardens front and back and a beautiful sort of suburban-type setting. So it was really Paul who was the working-class hero, not John, in actual fact.

Paul has always kept his roots with Liverpool more than any other member of The Beatles, right from the start until now. He has contributed specifically in getting the talent school going – he put lots of effort and lots of time into that, and he had to fight and battle to get it done, because that's what you have to do in Liverpool to get anything done. For some reason there's some barriers against anything happening there. But Paul did it, and he has always been visiting Liverpool, right throughout his life, no matter how famous he got, he was always back with is family, making it to all the get-togethers at Christmas and the parties with the relatives and everything. He is always chatting and meeting people he knew from the early days, more so than the others. Paul's always had his feet on the ground, and it shows in the way he brought up his family. They are a family who have got roots and there's no real problems with the McCartney family.

I always found, right from the very beginning, from the early Liverpool days, that Paul McCartney was the perfect PR man. It was Paul who was a driving force all the time. When we started *Mersey Beat* it was Paul who used to write to me,

you know, when they were abroad or making trips or anything. It was him who used to bring the photographs to me. I even remember one time when we were going down to the Cavern and Paul was in the queue and he called to me and said he had some photographs of Germany and gave me the pictures. He'd brought them down specially.

He has always been conscious and aware of the need to communicate with the media and he's always been the one who had tried to help the media, for the benefit of the group, whereas the others sometimes disliked the media, or were not bothered, couldn't be bothered with interviews.

"Paul has always kept his roots with Liverpool more than any other members of The Beatles, right from the start until now"

Paul always used to write to keep me up to date with everything that was happening. I found his letters were very funny and he had a sense of humour which was a bit similar to John's sense of humour. He used to write and describe Hamburg as a sort of Blackpool but with strip clubs. When he went to Paris and wrote about their visit to Olympia there was actual humour in it and the way he wrote was very funny and almost surreal-istic in style. It was a pity that he didn't develop that in the way that John did in his books.

Paul will be remembered for a very long time because he'll keep creating, I think, in the future. But he has created more than any other musician in this or the last century.

Bill Harry:
"Paul always used to write to keep me up to date with everything that was happening."

"Paul has created more than any other musician in the last century."

"PAUL AND JOHN WERE SO COOL. THEY BECAME THE PATHFINDERS FOR A GENERATION"

Roger McGuinn, singer and guitarist with the Byrds

The Byrds went to see *Hard Day's Night*. We had listened to The Beatles' records and we liked the whole way they came across. I had been working in the Brill Building in New York writing songs for Bobby Darin and really, then, I was a folk singer who liked rock music. After hearing The Beatles, I became a rock musician who could play folk. They changed the whole music scene.

I remember saying to other musicians around the village in New York, they are great stuff, they aren't bubble gum, listen to those passing chords, sheer beauty. Their impact was massive and immediate. There have been three main artists in popular music: Frank Sinatra, Elvis and The Beatles, and their impact was the greatest. They changed everything that followed, all those thousands of bands in their garages all over America all came from The Beatles.

In 1965 we toured England and Paul invited us to his club, The Scotch Of St James's. He sent a limo to pick us up. He said he had been listening to our music. We were blown away. He took us for a ride through London in his Aston Martin, at great speed. He was really hip, and he and John were so tight it was like one person at times. Unlike The Byrds, Crosby would just leave you out to dry, The Beatles all defended each other to the hilt. If you criticised, say, George then they would all respond.

After leaving the English tour, on the way home we wrote a song about the whole trip and being up there in the aeroplane and we knew it was about six miles high – 36,000 feet or so – but Gene Clark said let's change it to "Eight Miles High", it sounds better, more like "Eight Days A Week" by The Beatles. It just showed how much they influenced everyone.

Later when The Beatles toured the States and were staying in the Gabor mansion on Mulholland Drive in Los Angeles, they invited us up there. The trails up to the mansion were littered with kids camping out trying to get a glimpse. It was a crazy scene. Paul and John were so cool at that time, and it wasn't that Paul was just the safe tunesmith type of thing; they were both really edgy, trying things and experimenting with their lyrics, with their lifestyle, with everything. They became the pathfinders for a generation.

When we first met The Beatles we could tell they were really interested in our scene. It was amazing for us, we felt so humble compared to their success – I mean, people asked us if there was some kind of intercontinental rivalry there and we said, "No way! Those guys are on a different level to everyone else." But they were keen to tap into the lyrical side of what we were doing, especially with Bob Dylan. We introduced Paul to Dylan and he sort of challenged them to get more meaningful with their lyrics. I can remember spending long evenings and nights in darkened rooms just talking with Paul and John and Dylan.

Of course just as they had changed the whole way people wrote songs, they also changed the record industry. Before *Sgt Pepper* and *Revolver*, the business was all about singles. They changed that and made the album the focus. That changed the whole way we came to think about what we were doing and introduced the idea of the concept album, and linking songs and thoughts together and putting in deeper, more interesting ideas. The focus on the album grew when they stopped touring – that was one of Paul's greatest gifts to our culture.

Roger McGuinn: "After hearing The Beatles I became a rock musician who could play folk. They changed the whole music scene."

Peter Asher, brother of Jane Asher, record producer and former recording artist as part of the duo Peter & Gordon

I was very much aware of The Beatles, so I was as impressed and pleased to meet him as anybody would be. I like him, he seemed like a good chap. One forms early impressions cautiously.

I didn't hear Paul actually write very much in my presence as such. Certainly there were songs he had finished that he would then play to me, or he'd play me half-finished songs and stuff, which was very impressive.

The most memorable occasion was when he and John were together – and they didn't always write together. They were using my mother's music room in the basement and they had finished the song and had asked if I would come down to hear it. And I did and that was "I Wanna Hold Your Hand". They sat next to each other on the front of the little upright piano and sang it – and even without the benefit of historical perspective, it was clearly a very good song, and they sounded incredibly good singing live in a room together.

I remember subsequently going to hear some of their BBC recordings and being there when they were just rehearsing. They sang really loud, which you had to then, because there were no monitors, so to hear yourself you had to sing pretty loud and they sounded terrific. They were a remarkably well-matched pair of voices.

I don't remember it very well but we used to find ways of getting Paul out of the back of the house and stuff (while he was living with us). I believe my father once took him out over the roof or something, but I don't remember that myself. Certainly it was an inconvenience when my father [a doctor] was seeing patients and stuff – there would be fans gathered around the front door. There were aspects about having him as a house guest that were not convenient in the most practical sense, but in every other respect he really was the perfect guest.

Gordon and I had been working in a club called the Pickwick club and it was one of many gigs, we used to play a pub at lunch-time and this kind of thing – different stuff. And I was in my second year at King's College London, reading Philosophy, and Gordon was finishing or had just finished at Westminster, which is where we met – because he's a year younger than me. And … one night an A&R man called Norman Newell from EMI heard us and after we'd finished our set, in the traditional fashion, he invited us over for a drink and said, "Have you boys ever thought about making a record? Would you like to come and audition?" We said, "Absolutely yes."

So about a week later we were at EMI studios as it was then, it wasn't called Abbey Road then. And we recorded several songs as demos. Now it so happened that a week or so before this I had heard a song of Paul's that he'd played to us, which was "World Without Love" – without a bridge – and he said nothing much was happening to it because I believe they'd offered it to Billy J Kramer who didn't like it. And John didn't like it – I think he thought that the song was too wimpy for The Beatles.

At that time I knew I might be able to get hold of this other song that I think we could sing well, and at this point in evolution of the music business you weren't committed to making an

"THERE IS NO ONE THAT HAS NOT BEEN INFLUENCED BY PAUL. I THINK PAUL'S POSITION IN THE ROCK PANTHEON IS CLEARLY ASSURED"

album – it was like, "Let's cut a couple of singles and see what happens." And we might easily have done that – and cut two songs that were just average and gone no further.

So I then I said to Paul, "By the way, we've got a record contract and what are the chances of you being able to finish that song and let us do it?" And he said, "Fine." And then couple of times I had to nag him, I remember, to actually write the bridge, which is a very good bridge when he did. So he gave us the song, and we did it and of course in retrospect it was stunning, the fact was, our very first record was No.1 all over the world.

Then, at the time, with that 60s youthful enthusiasm, you kind of go, "Oh, so that's how it works." You get a good song and make a record and it comes out and it's a No.1 hit", and it seemed extremely natural. And now I realise, God knows more than ever, being in the business I'm in now, it's a one in a million chance and we were exceptionally lucky. And certainly we owe Paul a great deal of gratitude because who is to say, had we not done that song, what else we might have done, and how well it might have done?

My mother's music room was downstairs where I mentioned they wrote "I Wanna Hold Your Hand". I believe he wrote "Yesterday" in his room upstairs, because "Yesterday" was a guitar song, not a piano song. And he had guitars in his room – next to mine – at the top of the house, so my guess would be that he probably wrote "Yesterday" up there. I remember him writing it, and I remember it having no words, though I was not present for the "scrambled eggs" story that I've heard subsequently, though I believe my mother was at the time. She remembered him singing it and him having the provisional lyric of "scrambled eggs" because he just wanted that –

the "da-da-da", but without words. But I do remember hearing that when it was a wordless melody and being impressed. And then hearing it again when he'd finished it and being extremely impressed by it.

"I think Paul is as highly respected as anyone can be in rock & roll. And adored, let's say, as much as you can possibly be without being dead."

I think Paul is as highly respected as anyone can possibly be in rock & roll. And adored – revered – let's say as much as you can be without being dead, you know. But that's the only way – you have to be Elvis or John Lennon to get a higher degree of respect. It's really hard still to be around – it's always been true in classical music and everything – and you finally get your absolute full-on admiration when you die, and that's certainly not worth it.

There is no-one that has not been influenced by Paul McCartney, and the same people have been influenced by Buddy Holly, but as I say, when Buddy's dead it puts a whole other picture on it. And I think, views may differ on Paul's later work – some people love it, some people don't – he was falsely accused of writing some soppy songs when he has actually written some classic rock & roll songs – very intense rock & roll songs, and he's a great rock & roll singer. So I think Paul's position in the rock pantheon is clearly assured."

Donovan: "Paul may have encouraged the classical side of The Beatles."

Donovan, British singer–songwriter and friend of The Beatles

The year 1966 was really popping for me and they were already big, and so it was difficult to actually see each other because of all of the fame. But the recollection is that in '66 we still had time on our hands – how I don't know. But on one sweet summer day in London – I had a flat in Maida Vale, Paul had the place around St John's Wood – and he called in.

At the time I had a little tape recorder and I was writing songs all the time as I do, and I knew he wrote songs all the time. The doorbell rang, I was on my own, it was maybe a Sunday – I don't remember any cars in the street. And it was Paul. He came in and said he had a new song he wanted to play me. He sat down. At the time I had these Japanese tatami mats on the floor and a brass bed – I mean, I had my influences a bit mixed up there – it was Victor an bohemia mixed up with Japanese philosophy.

Still, we were sitting on the floor and he played me this song, which was a song he called "Orla Matungi". "Orla Matungi, blowing his mind in the dark with a pipe full of clay, what can you say?" And as a description of the beginning of a song, these were not the words that would end up being the opening to "Eleanor Rigby", but songwriters often do this – you fill it in later, like an artist fills in a sketch.

So that was interesting, and I played him one of my new songs and then the doorbell rang. What I'm going to describe to you shows a bit how Paul and The Beatles were held in reverence in those days, which blew me away – the doorbell rang, I opened the door, it was a young bobby, a cop. And Paul came up behind me and leaned over my shoulder to see who it was and when the young policeman saw it was Paul McCartney, he stood to attention and saluted and said, "Oh it's you Mr McCartney". I turned around and looked at Paul and I went, "My God". And we turned back and looked at the cop and he said, "Is that your car in the street?" An Aston Martin, with one wheel parked on the pavement? And the door open and the radio on? And Paul said, "Yeah I think it is". And he said, "Would you like me to park it for you?" And Paul gave him the keys and he went down, parked the car and came back, gave us the keys.

The door shut and we sat down, we didn't say much about it. I just said to myself, "Wow, that's it. The Beatles are like royalty." We got back to the serious world of songwriting and he took out the song that he'd been working on called "Yellow Submarine". Now he knew I had an interest in writing children's songs, he knew that from listening to my material, and he came up with this melody and he came up with the words and he said he's missing one line.

Of course I looked at him and said to myself, "McCartney's missing a line of a song?". I didn't know until later that there were gaps in Beatles songs filled in for whatever reason by whoever was around. So I was obviously charmed by this and said, "Wait a minute!" And I went into another room, took the guitar out and came back with a line. And it's not the most devastating line in the world but I modelled it on the rest of the song and it was, "Sky of blue and sea of green" – that's it – "In my yellow submarine".

So that's it – fits wonderfully. And so that was

"WITHOUT PAUL McCARTNEY IN THE WORLD, WE'D HAVE TO INVENT HIM"

the collaboration, and from then on we enjoyed each other's company and I visited him at his house. Recently, somebody sent me a bootleg CD of me and Paul – it's a CD bootleg, you can buy it – and it's the sessions we did in his basement in St John's Wood. Paul met Linda Eastman, and Linda had a little girl, Heather. So when I would go round to St John's Wood I kind of naturally would want to sing to the kids as I had begun to sing to my little baby boy at the time – and other children whenever they were around. Woody Guthrie wrote children's songs, and I was influenced by that and so I wrote children's songs myself. And when I was growing up my father wrote me an enormous amount of children's poetry, and so when we were doing those sessions, Paul had already begun to write for children, particularly for Heather.

In the days that we are talking about there was still time to see each other and hang out – it seemed like life hadn't got to such a pace and so we visited each other's sessions. And there may have been so few going on really, in the London area, that you knew where everybody was at any particular time, and *A Day In The Life* was extraordinary and I did wander in and out. I guess I was in a kind of solo mood but I did wander through and saw what was happening and it was extraordinary. I mean, to see all the orchestra completely made up for a classical concert.

Paul may have even encouraged the classical side of The Beatles more than John or George. Paul was very much the kind of conductor, he loved the whole idea of *A Day In The Life* becoming so huge, this extraordinary sound. It was a happening – if I had to describe that recording session, it was a happening.

As a songwriter who I feel is not finished yet

– I don't think the legacy's over – I think there's more to come, there's something yet to come. But on a more sombre note there comes a time in an artist's life when his super-fame casts a shadow into his future, which is very hard to beat,

The impact of Paul and the impact of The Beatles – what would we be without them? Maybe I'll paraphrase Lionel Bart when he said something about an extraordinary event that happened. He said of this event, "If it hadn't happened, we would have had to invent it." Which is Lionel Bart's very clever way of saying, "We need that – without it we are not who we are." And if a poet can be described as somebody who in one line can focus on a new way of looking at one's life, then we can't do without The Beatles, we can't do without Paul McCartney in this century.

But they weren't the only movers of change, they weren't the only heralds and they weren't the only poet–musicians. But they were the most popular and Paul continues to kind of be, I suppose, he's the continuing light of that extraordinary event and without Paul McCartney in the world, we'd have to invent him.

Paul's very prolific as a songwriter. In fact if he fell on the piano, by the time he had picked himself up, he would have written three songs.

I had to say that because it's true. I mean I've seen a guitar fall over and it just goes baaaaang and that's, you know, "A Hard Day's Night".

> "I don't think the legacy's over – I think there's more to come, there's something yet to come"

Donovan with The Beatles in Rishikesh. "The Beatles are like royalty."

"HE HAS SO MUCH MUSIC IN HIM, HE SEEMS LIKE HE NEVER RUNS OUT OF IDEAS. HE IS TOTALLY UNIQUE"

Brian Wilson, singer and songwriter with The Beach Boys

The first time I heard The Beatles was when I heard "I Want to Hold Your Hand" and instantly I was totally aware of their power, the instant electricity, and I was jealous. Mike [Love] and I went for dinner and all we could talk about was what we were going to do about these Beatles.

I got totally into *Rubber Soul*. At the time we were all smoking a lot of marijuana and that album and marijuana became linked, they became as one for me and I decided that somehow I needed to top the achievement of *Rubber Soul*. It became like a competition. I wanted to make an album that could make people happy like *Rubber Soul*. I needed to produce something as good as that. It was the first time I had heard a record that had a wholeness to it – the whole record meant something.

I must have listened to Rubber Soul maybe 35 times one after another and then I began to make the *Pet Sounds* album ... the music just fell out of my hands and I've got The Beatles and Paul McCartney to thank for that.

Not only did their music get to me, but the voices of John and Paul made a huge impact. They were so real, so true to life ... I started to feel a deep connection with Paul, it got really deep at around the *Let It Be* time. That song meant a lot to me, for the people in the world who are maybe scared or lonely, they need to just let it be, relax just for a moment, it'll be OK.

Do I love Paul McCartney's melodies? I love his melodies, are you kidding? His melodies are amazing. I was so nervous when he came to visit me. It was 1967 and I was in the studio, we were all eating vegetables to get in the mood for the music we were making, and he walked in and he was looking so cool. He was wearing these red patent leather shoes and this white suit and, yes, he just looked the coolest. He just sat there and chewed on a carrot and then he played 'She's Leaving Home' from *Sgt Pepper* on the piano, and my wife cried and it was such a moving thing.

As a bass player Paul McCartney is technically fantastic, but his harmonies and the psychological thing he brings to the music comes through. Psychologically he is really strong. Sometimes I would listen to what he has done and it would scare me, his music is so powerful.

The other thing that I could never get was how versatile he was. How did he get the time to write and make such different music? In the morning he would serve up 'She's Leaving Home', for lunch 'Hey Jude', and then 'Get Back' for dinner, that's a recipe for success! But he is so versatile, we would spend ages trying to work out where he got all those different types of songs from. It came from a whole bunch of places.

There came a while when I thought that our connection meant that we were sort of carrying a load together. It was cool, but the baggage was heavy and for some of the time it would be him and then it would be me trying to carry the music forward. After a while you get tired and have to say, here, you take it. But Paul McCartney has kept on going. He has so much music in him, it seems like he never runs out of ideas. He is totally unique.

"I wanted to make an album that could make people happy like *Rubber Soul*"

Brian Wilson:
"The thing I could never get was how versatile he was."

Michael Lindsay-Hogg, director of the film *Let It Be*

I got a call from Brian Epstein's office about doing the video for "Paperback Writer". In those days it's hard to believe now the power The Beatles had as four individuals, because of their fame and celebrity and their talent and the way they'd taken over the world. I met them at Abbey Road and they asked me for dinner. Unlike most rock & roll dinners, which would be pizzas coming in, they were in a dining room with linen, silverware, wine glasses – a full meal. There were only six chairs in the room, occupied by The Beatles, Mal Evans and Neil Aspinal, and the only other sitting object was a little hassock, or pouf, which I sat on. The only problem was that I was so low down my chin rested on the table. As I pitched my ideas to them I felt disadvantaged – perhaps that was their design.

I got a call from Paul, I think, or a guy who used to be involved in the [Apple] movie company called Dennis O'Dell. And they said they had these songs, "Revolution" and "Hey Jude", and that Paul wanted someone who was good with drapes and a wind machine. That was the first brief for 'Hey Jude'. Then we talked. One of the problems with "Hey Jude" was the four-minute closing chorus. What are you going to show? You can't just show them all the time or it would run out of steam. So Paul and I had this idea that after the verse, The Beatles should be joined by what looked like the world. Not just the conventional rock & roll world of kids, but housewives, the postmen – people who represented all walks of life. And so we set about getting extras.

The one I talked to mainly about that one was Paul, he was the one who was interested at that time. Educated and literate he is, but I think, obviously his greatest gifts are his musical gift and his angel's voice, as well as his songwriting. If we decided that an idea would make sense Paul would then want to follow that idea, he's very thorough and persistent.

I think it still was a version of a democracy at the time, a top-heavy democracy, with John and Paul being kind of the head democrats. If it was going to be anything strange it would go to the group vote, but basically for "Hey Jude" it was Paul – and for "Revolution" it was John. When we shot "Revolution", which was a performance, it was John I spoke to most. He said that the biggest close-up should be on "If you go talking about Chairman Mao, you're not gonna make it with anyone anyhow" because that was the most important lyric of the song. I think they were starting in those days to diverge. There were Paul's songs and the things that Paul was interested in and John's songs and the projects John was interested in.

Paul was the one who called me about *Let It Be*. When we were at Twickenham shooting "Hey Jude", we did four or five takes. In between the takes, to fill in the time, The Beatles would play, riff-play, do old Motown, and there was the audience there – the hundred or so people we bused in as extras for "Hey Jude". So for the first time since they stopped touring they were actually playing to an audience. And they liked that, the audience was affectionate and friendly, not trying to rip their clothes off. They had a good buzz doing that. So they thought, is there any way they could play to an audience again in a way which worked for them. So as a result of this, the germ of the idea that became "Let It Be" was born.

Michael Lindsay-Hogg: "It's hard to believe now the power The Beatles had as four individuals."

"PAUL WOULD BE THE ONE WHO CAME ON FOOT... AND THE OTHERS WOULD ARRIVE IN THEIR MERCEDES AND ROLLS"

It was originally supposed to be a TV special. One of them wanted to do the special at the Cavern, as a pay-back to their first fans. I wanted to do it in an amphitheatre on the coast of Tunisia, which Paul and John liked. We even sent an advance team to Tunisia. The plan was to get on a boat, rehearse on the boat, bringing a lot of the audience with us, a funny boat jamboree. It was a very heady idea, but that's the sort of thing they could accomplish, both with their finances and their position. But Ringo didn't really want to do it and George wanted to get the album right first. His point, rightly, was that they were musicians first and they weren't actors.

So then a few days went by and we all sat around at Twickenham, waiting to see what was going to happen. Paul and John and Ringo and Yoko, who was with John all the time, and Linda, who was starting to figure in Paul's life. And they would be visited, like royalty, by other royalty, like Peter Sellers and they'd do funny voices – all waiting to see what would happen with this enterprise that would be *Let It Be*. Also what was going to happen with The Beatles. No-one really thought they would break up at the time because they'd had quarrels before. But I think there were larger issues happening, particularly between George and Paul and John.

I think Paul very much wanted to keep The Beatles together, and John was pulling another way. I think that George was disturbed that if there were, say, 12 cuts on an album, 10 would be Lennon and McCartney songs, one would be a fish thrown to Ringo and one would be his song. He was wanting more artistic and financial say.

I remember when we got to Apple [to shoot the rest of the film], Paul would be the one who came on foot. When we were shooting the arrivals at Apple, someone would say they'd seen Paul, he'd be walking up from Savile Row, or Burlington Arcade, and then the others would arrive in their Mercedeses and Rollses. Maybe Paul came by bus, maybe he came by cab.

Going up to the roof was an idea which came in the last week or so of filming. I, and a few guys on the crew, were getting weary of the rehearsals – even though it was The Beatles! It was like a Sartre drama that we couldn't get out of. So one Saturday we were up in the boardroom, and they all were there, and my version of what happened – I say my version, because subsequently everybody has claimed credit for the suggestion – what I said was, look we've got to finish this somehow, if you won't go to Tunisia, why don't we just do it on the roof. They said OK. So after lunch Paul and Mal Evans and I went up on the roof and looked around, Paul jumped around to see what the acoustics were like, and we looked for camera angles. And then he said, yeah, that would work, so we were going to do it the following Thursday, but the weather was bad so we did it on Friday, which was the end of January '69.

The Beatles being true to their characters at the time they were supposed to go up at 12.30 and they didn't agree until 12.20. They were fighting downstairs in the boardroom, Paul wanted to do it, George didn't, Ringo didn't care and so John said, "Fuck it, let's go and do it". So they walked up the narrow staircase onto the roof and into history. That was their last performance to any kind of public. It became obvious when we were cutting *Let It Be* that they were not going to be together any more, and that's why I ended it with John's line, "I hope we passed the audition", because if anybody ever did, they did.

Neil Innes, writer and singer with The Bonzo Dog Doo-Dah Band and co-creator of Beatles pastiche band The Rutles

I first met Paul on the *Magical Mystery Tour* film set. The Bonzos had been coerced into doing their number for the film in [London strip club] Raymond's Revue Bar. It was a very pleasant day and all the boys had heard Gorilla [The Bonzos' new album] and Paul was very complimentary about the music. Paul was very much at the helm and I liked that idea. Paul took on the artistic spirit of those days – everyone had seen an Orson Welles film or they'd seen a bit of a Magritte painting, and all those influences melded together.

The Bonzos had been nagged for ages by the record company to come up with a single – so finally I came up with this song called "Urban Spaceman", largely because of being on the road and seeing all the embryonic one-way systems and all the same shops. We were referring to these developments as urban spaces, and I thought, "Oh I guess that makes me an urban spaceman". So I had a half title and I had a day off and I wrote it in the afternoon. It had five verses and Viv [Vivian Stanshall, the Bonzos' leader] said that was too many so we cut it down to three and part of the story is that our producer and manager was of the old school, if you like. You would only have two hours on this, and then it's time to move on to the next track. Being an unruly bunch of art students we said, "Oh I haven't finished, I've got a lot more ideas, you know." And our producer was bemoaning this to Paul down in, probably, the Speakeasy, a famous drinking hole in those days.

And Paul said, "Well, I'll come and produce it."

So that's the way … we could get this track off the control knobs as it were. And funnily enough, because it was a time issue, when Paul arrived he was sort of very relaxed and saying, "How are you?" … and sat down at the piano and started playing these lovely chords and singing "Hey Jude, don't make it bad." It's a very long song and he's singing it as though he'd just written it – no one actually knew that it was "Hey Jude", because it obviously came out much later. I was getting the giggles because I could see the manager going "Humph" and looking at his watch and this and that, but how could he interrupt the great man?

Paul was brilliant and he was very kind to me because I wasn't the main singer and he made me sing the song through. And Larry [Smith, drummer] was tapping away a kind of energetic version on the drums and Paul said, "We'll double-track the drums." So that unique kind of McCartney feel came through into the production.

Again, to irritate the management, it had taken eight hours, but at least we had Paul McCartney's name on the thing and this is when we brought out our coup de grace. We said, "We don't want Paul's name on the record." "What?" "Well, no, we think that as artists our record ought to make it in its own right, under our name."

And of course Paul was set up for this. They said, "Well what are you going to put on there then?" We said, "Apollo C Vermouth". Even though Gus Dudgeon did the final mix, it is all Paul's musicianship and flair. The record did actually start to sell, it got to about 17, I think, after about five or six weeks, and then the management couldn't stand it anymore and they leaked the fact that Paul had produced and it shot up to No. 5.

Neil Innes:
"The thing about Paul as a songwriter is that he's the one who knew the rules."

"I THINK PAUL WAS POLITELY ENTHUSIASTIC ABOUT THE RUTLES, BUT I THINK IT WAS A THOROUGH IRRITATION AT THE TIME"

During the course of the recording Paul picked up Viv's ukelele and, even though he's left-handed, he started playing it and he was one of those musicians who could pick up a couple of bricks and make them sound good. I'm jealous of that wonderful ability to do that. Anyway, he's plinking away and the manager's wife came over and said, "Oh, what's that you've got there, a poor man's violin?" And Paul replied, "No, it's a rich man's ukelele." It was the lads versus the establishment really. And he was really very kind and very helpful.

The thing about Paul as a songwriter is that he's the one who knew the rules. You've got to get somebody's interest in three seconds or you might as well not bother and then you ring all the changes. He had an innate sort of sense of pop art. He had all these kind of artistic – not pretensions – but sympathies, if you like.

You didn't stay on anything too long, you brought in a lovely sound or you changed the chord and things like that. And when I came to write *The Rutles*, I thought if I start listening to The Beatles stuff I'm doomed! So I thought back to art school, when I first heard "Love Me Do" and things like that, and I thought, what was I doing at that time? So I started to write, sort of, songs that were about what I was going through, like, "Hold My Hand" and "I Must Be In Love", which were the hardest in fact to write.

Going on to the psychedelic theme you can have a lot more fun with words, but I didn't listen to any of their songs until my songs, *The Rutles* songs, had been written and then we listened to their productions. It had bongos and things that I'd never heard before and it was a labour of love, musically, for everybody involved on *The Rutles* album project, both of them. You know, it's our tribute to Paul and the boys. We rehearsed the songs in someone's house while Wimbledon was on and we'd do a few tracks and then watch a bit of tennis, over two weeks. And we felt like we'd been a band on the road and we went into the studio and the album only took three weeks. But there were so many out-takes … there was a thing that never made it on the first album called "We've Arrived And To Prove It We're Here". It's infectious because you can hear the fun that was being had, you know?

I think Paul was politely enthusiastic about *The Rutles*, but I think it was a thorough irritation actually at the time because unbeknown to us we'd put out *The Ruttles* album at the same time he'd brought out [Wings album] *London Town*. And every press thing he went to everyone was saying, "What do you think of *The Rutles*?" until he needed all his kind of equanimity if you like, to sort of smile his way through it and point out he had got an album of his own. And in fact after he'd been so helpful to Bonzos and to me, I thought it was a rotten thing to happen.

And years later, about three or four years ago at a party at George's, I managed to sort of say to Paul, "I'm really sorry the albums came out at the same time" – and after a little misunderstanding in which I was genuinely trying to say that wasn't meant to happen, he said: "That's all under the bridge now." But all of them gave permission to use the footage to make *The Ruttles* – look what it did – I mean it was almost a kind of official biography, you know. It needed to come out because people were going crazy about them all getting back together again. And George thought that this would diffuse the situation, poke a bit of fun at it.

In the future I hope people will see him as a great guy, great artist and a great musician.

Steve Miller, songwriter, musician and collaborator with Paul McCartney

I was working in Olympic Studios back in February 1969 with Glynn Johns, and Glynn was working at the same time with The Beatles on the *Get Back/Let It Be* sessions. They were over-running so I had a couple of days to wait and Glynn suggested that I went in one day to see what the band was doing.

So the next day I turned up, and when I pushed open the door there was John and Paul recording what we all came to know as *Get Back*. They were laying down the vocals. I was like a fly on the wall just watching the most creative people I could think of at work. They were so gracious and so relaxed they made me welcome. They sort of had their own way of communicating. Hardly anything was spoken, they just knew what the other wanted or was getting at and they had the most amazing talent.

The next day I went along some time in the afternoon and this time John had failed to turn up. George hung around for a while but then left, leaving just Paul. The guitars and the amps were all set up so we just began to jam a bit. He was on drums and I played guitar and, like, straight away I could sort of communicate with him.

I told him about this song I was about to record, "My Dark Hour" for the *Brave New World* record. And he said, "Let's do it", and it just sort of happened. He's on drums beating hell out of them and I'm on guitar, and then he plays bass and I'm on rhythm. We were popping tracks over and using the techniques that the Beatles had developed for multitracking. Seven hours later and

it's done, and he just sort of walks out of the door. But he did really beat hell out of those drums.

It was hard to believe it having seen John and Paul together the day before, but they were going through hell in their business life. They had just learned that Brian Epstein's mother had sold off their publishing after his death. Then, that day, they had met and voted that Allan Klein would be their business manager. Now unlike the others, Paul did not want that.

I thought I am just a little guy in this industry but I have my own publishing, I own my masters, but they have none of that. They have just lost a body of work unlike anyone else's, unrivalled, and someone is walking away with it. And now they are suggesting having Allan Klein who is basically like a thief-as-manager. He is like an old-style music manager who is out to fleece the artist, so no wonder that Paul is frustrated.

Paul told me that he just did not want to put his life and his work in Klein's hands. It's impossible to guess what he must have felt like, seeing that amazing body of work taken away. [Author's note: At the same meeting that appointed Klein, Allan Klein said that he could not allow The Beatles to bid directly for Northern Songs as it would cost too much. This was totally at odds with McCartney's desire to buy the catalogue and therefore own their own publishing. That meeting took place on February 3rd 1969, the same day as he recorded the track "My Dark Hour" with Steve Miller. McCartney appears on the Steve Miller album *Brave New World* under the pseudonym of Paul Ramon].

Paul was an awesome musical presence. He was, like, ten feet tall with music and it was everything: folk, rock, music hall, choral, it was all there. He was like a different animal with Lennon.

Steve Miller:
"Paul was an awesome musical presence. He was, like, ten feet tall with music."

"HE IS SO GENEROUS AND SO POSITIVE, AND I THINK THAT'S WHY SOME OF THE PRESS FIND IT EASY TO HAVE A GO AT HIM"

When they were together they became something else, more than just the two of them together. That communication was incredible. It was like two high-speed computers just fizzing between each other. I felt like a nobody, so humbled to be in their presence, but Paul had obviously listened to my records, he knew the albums and discussed them. The Beatles had a massive impact on me as a musician; they had an impact on everyone.

The first impact of The Beatles was with their writing. It was the sheer quality of it and there was so much, and it came so fast. They took rock & roll and opened it out; they showed us what possibilities there were. Then they took recording, the actual act of making the records, and they totally changed that. When I first made a record, they gave me three hours to record a song and a couple of days to do an album and that was it. TV, well there was the *Ed Sullivan Show* where you might see some musician, but it was very mainstream. They went on that and showed that there was a massive audience for the new music. Something like 60 million Americans watched that show. It was the Beatles who took music into the 60s and helped kill the square 50s. They put all that old stuff to rest.

Between 1964 and 1967 they grew so much, each album was better and more interesting than the last, they brought in new influences and they took us on that journey with them. We just did not know what to expect next and they never let us down. They added classic inspirations via George Martin, they took us to India. Can you imagine that most people had never heard of meditation let alone transcendental meditation, and they took us there too?

Can you imagine what it was like when they first came to America? They were followed around by 300 guys with microphones and flashbulbs and they never disappointed, they always exceeded expectations, they were funny, they were clever and they were good. There was an intellectual quality to their music that gave them a depth … in front of all this attention, all this expectation, they bloomed.

Before The Beatles no-one played football stadiums, now I've played hundreds of stadiums, but they were the first. Elvis had been sort of cool, but he was also sort of weird. He had gone off to Vegas, made movies, got fat. The Beatles just kept pushing the boundaries. They changed everything and they changed it with talent.

There has never been a group as popular either, so they were taking this massive audience on a life-changing trip.

I then worked again with Paul a few years back and we wrote and recorded some songs together and, you know, I realised that The Beatles were so important to him, he was sort of shy outside of them because, unlike me, who played in all sorts of bands with all sorts of musicians, for Paul there had really only been The Beatles for a long time. They were his band.

And you know, despite all the spotlight and the attention over the years, he has maintained his love and passion for music and for people. He is so generous and so positive, and I think that's why some elements of the press find it easy to have a go at him, because for cynics he is a great target, someone who is trying to make the world a better place.

"It was like two high-speed computers just fizzing between each other"

"AND I LOVED THE SOUND OF THEIR VOICES – DENNY AND PAUL AND LINDA HAD A MAGICAL SOUND"

Steve Holly, drummer in the last Wings line-up

When I was invited to go and audition at the London offices, he was a couple of hours late getting there and by that time I was a mess. Sweaty palms – I'd never been so scared! I think it's intimidating meeting him whoever you are, whenever you meet him. I still get that feeling all these years later, it's crazy.

It was one of the things I think we shared in common – not only a love of the drums and music in general, but I had a lot of respect for the way he played, and for Ringo.

The bass playing was the thing that just blew my mind, and always had done, so that opportunity was absolutely my favourite part of playing with Paul. He's the best. I don't think there's anyone that can touch him, I truly believe that. He would not just be playing roots, but very often he'd be playing harmony to a vocal line, or contributing something that added to another part of the song altogether. There are very few bass players that do that.

It always occurred to me that the Wings Over America tour was so successful and a great band. And I wonder how much of that was repetitious for him and I felt even during the UK dates that perhaps, I'd walk off stage elated, saying, "That was great" and he'd say, "It was OK". So I think maybe it didn't rise to what he wanted, realise his expectations. I thought we might be able to turn it around in Japan, but we never found out and that was a horrible disappointment for me. I didn't believe it at first. We had just come through customs, I had come in from London, and I believe Paul and Lawrence [Juber, guitarist] had

come in from New York and we'd cleared customs and were sitting on the bus waiting to go to the hotel. I checked into the hotel, had a snack, a little nap and the phone rang, and it was Linda saying, "Paul's been busted" and I said, "yeah, sure Linda, see you later, very funny". "No, no it's real". I remember getting dressed and going downstairs and when the doors opened – pop, pop, 60 cameras go at once. I could see all the crew had long faces. It was terribly disappointing.

Linda was an incredible influence and a beautiful person who took so much abuse, I couldn't believe it sometimes. We had a great relationship, I cared a lot for her and I loved the sound of their voices – Denny and Paul and Linda singing together had a magical sound. She obviously kept him so well grounded, it's very rare to see people who love each other that much to start with, and in that business and to maintain that relationship through so many difficult times – that commands respect. It's a tragedy that she's gone, it broke my heart a lot more than I expected it to. She was a very special person.

What's incredible to me is that with the amount I've been exposed to these songs, I never tire of them, there's always something new to find. We're talking a long period of listening now, and it's still fascinating to me.

I recently watched a band at a local club that call themselves Fab Faux – some of the finest musicians in New York and they played a two-hour, twenty minute set of Beatles music. It's not easy to do – the songs do not play themselves, you really have to know what you're doing. It's just astounding to me how powerful those songs are, even handled that way, as great as it was, it's still not as great as The Beatles ever were. Tremendous, powerful – very important.

Steve Holly:
"The bass playing was the thing that just blew my mind. He's the best. I don't think there's anyone that can touch him."

The **Wings Over America** *line-up. Clockwise from left: Paul McCartney, Denny Laine, Steve Holly, Lawrence Juber, Linda McCartney.*

George Martin
"Paul has great
understanding of
orchestral colour."

George Martin, The Beatles' record producer

They were a very attractive group of men. I like them so much because of their wacky sense of humour. They were different, they were irreverent, not too respectful. It wasn't their music that attracted me because I didn't think it was all that brilliant. It was unusual, but it was their style, and I think they also in turn were prepared to like me because of the stuff I'd done with The Goons and people like that so we hit it off quite well.

What was lacking was the rhythm sounds. I mean, Paul gave a lovely bass sound but the drums didn't have what I thought was needed, and I said to Brian on the next session we did, "I don't mind what you do with the group, but I've got to make a good record and I'll book a drummer as I don't want to use your drummer." And for me it was just going to be a fake thing.

The first time I really worked seriously together with The Beatles in the studio was after the boys were determined to stop touring. They had all grown very tired of their goldfish bowl – they'd been doing it for four years on the trot. They wanted really to concentrate on their music and I was very grateful for this because I'd always been grabbing them at odd moments, and it was the only chance I had of working with them. Suddenly, with the beginning of *Strawberry Fields* and *Sgt Pepper*, suddenly we found ourselves with unlimited time in the studio and that was terrific because they all had ideas they wanted to express. Both John and Paul – I've always regarded them as being opposite complementary partners and geniuses – they both had ideas about what they wanted to do and they both

came up with some astonishing work, wonderful work. John showed us the idea of what he had for "A Day In The Life" (from the *Sgt Pepper* album) but he had no way of developing it, he had no idea of how it should be arranged and Paul was asked by John if he could help, you know, it was a real collaboration. John said, "Have you got anything I could use?" Paul didn't have much, he had another fragment which is the one we know, the middle, "Woke up, fell out of bed ..." and so on, and it had nothing to do with John's song at all, nothing at all. And Paul wisely then said, "Well, OK, let's put these bits together but let's not put them too close together, we'll separate them by 24 bars of rhythm which we'll fill in later." And it was a radical thought and I thought to myself, what the hell are we going to fill those 24 bars with? I thought it was a long time by anyone's standards, for a guitar solo or anything like that. And I asked them what they thought about it, and they wanted to use a symphony orchestra. They said, "If we get a symphony orchestra into the studio, we'll just tell them to play what we like."

Of course, you can't do that and I gently explained that to them. Paul went away and thought and came back with this wonderful, wacky idea of getting them to play a huge climax, starting with their lowest note, finishing with their highest note – over 24 bars – it was a revolutionary thought. It was Paul's idea to do that, and it made the song into something that was absolutely unique.

I think they were all incredibly inquisitive about what could be done. They were always coming to me, Paul in particular, and saying, "What sounds can you give us?" "What instruments don't we know about?" And of course he'd

"PAUL'S PLACE IN THE HISTORY OF MUSIC IS THERE FOREVER, HE IS ONE OF THE GREATEST MUSICIANS OF THE 20th CENTURY"

heard something on a television or radio programme. It was a Brandenberg Concerto – a very high trumpet sound which Bach used, a Bach trumpet. He came to me and said, "Great sound, can we use it?" I said, "Sure, you can if you want to". And that led to "Penny Lane".

Paul's always been a workaholic. I think even now he goes regularly to his studio every day and there's nothing wrong with that. Paul was the most organised of the quartet in terms of music and I think that Paul would have made a great arranger if he'd really set himself to it. But I guess he didn't need to do it. I wish he had done. I mean he was always frightened of learning music properly in case it took away something. He was frightened of losing that spark of originality. But he's got such good understanding of music, he's a profoundly good musician and he has a great understanding of orchestral colour, so that now I think that he is a fine composer in a classical sense – I think he's got that quality. But out of all the people I've worked with, he was the most articulate in terms of what he wanted.

When I heard "Yesterday" I said I couldn't think of Ringo playing heavy drums on it – it's much too gentle for that. I suggested strings and Paul said "I don't want Mantovani." I said, "Well it doesn't have to be Mantovani, it can be a string quartet" – very clinical. But when we did that and I started doing the score, I sat down with him and explained to him what I had in mind and he started putting little ideas in, which were great. There's a particular cello note – a cello bend in the second half when it goes to the seventh of a chord, which is very characteristic of Paul. It's not my idea – I wish it was, I wish I'd thought of that.

I think that what Paul did on *Abbey Road* was the best of the stuff that we did with The Beatles.

But it was Paul's work on the long one, particularly the end bit and the great "Golden Slumbers" which is a mixture of orchestral work and rock & roll – great ideas, everything in it, drum solos, guitar solos, super vocal and that's one of my favourite bits of Paul.

I think the great thing about The Beatles and Paul in particular is that they always gave me something new, they never gave me the old re-hash, they never gave me *Star Wars 2*. It was always a new brilliant piece of thinking.

I'm sure Paul does miss John. Their partnership was a strange one because it was built on love but also on rivalry, they were in competition with each other. But those elements combined to give the two of them each what individually they didn't necessarily have. Since John's death, Paul has collaborated with different people, he wrote with Elvis Costello for a bit. But it's never had quite the same fusion that he had with John. Of course, he's a fine writer in his own right anyway, he's done some great stuff. I think when *Flaming Pie* came out it was his best in a long time – there are some super songs on that. I was very honoured really, to work with him on those.

Paul's place in the history of music is there forever, he is one of the great musicians of the 20th century. John also occupies that place, he's up there with George Gershwin and Cole Porter in the popular music field. His presence is unassailable and his music will be heard into the middle of the next century and beyond.

"Paul was the most organised of the quartet in terms of music"

George Martin: "I think the great thing about The Beatles and Paul in particular is that they always gave me something new, they never gave me the old re-hash, they never gave me **Star Wars 2.***"*

George Martin: "… he's got such good understanding of music, he's a profoundly good musician."

Image from the rarely seen
footage of **The Beatles,** *held*
in the TSW archive,

& then

I met Paul McCartney for the first time at a central London pub called the Devonshire Arms in Duke Street, W1, just off Manchester Square where EMI Records used to have its office headquarters. During the early 60s the pub was a favourite haunt of EMI's rising stars. They would drop in to have one for the road after recording their promotional guest spots for the Radio Luxembourg shows EMI sponsored. Playing almost non-stop pop and rock music each evening, the continental station's English-language broadcasts beamed the era's only commercial radio programming into the UK, and paid-for plays of new releases on Luxembourg were considered to be very valuable in helping to boost singles into the Top 40.

My initial rendezvous with Paul and the other three Beatles came one evening in November 1962, a few weeks after their first single, "Love Me Do", had been released on EMI's Parlophone label. At this time the group's flamboyant young manager, Liverpool record and electrical retailer Brian Epstein, was in the process of persuading me to join his recently launched NEMS Enterprises management organisation to handle press and publicity, not only for The Beatles but also for a growing roster of other promising Merseyside bands and solo singers which he proposed to sign up in 1963, ranging from Cilla Black to Gerry And The Pacemakers. I had already put together a media publicity manual on The Beatles to go out to journalists and DJs with review copies of "Love Me Do". I intended this to be a one-off freelance job done at Epstein's request for a flat fee of £20 and so far I had resisted his offers of full-time work because I was perfectly happy where I was — occupying a small inconspicuous office in a quiet backwater at the Decca Record Company on London's Albert Embankment where I wrote the notes that appeared on the back of Decca Group LP album and EP covers. The job left me with ample time to spare for a little freelance work including a weekly record review column I did for *The Liverpool Echo*.

Apparently Epstein decided that if I met and got to know John Lennon, Paul, George Harrison and Ringo Starr, the power of their individual personalities and their collective charisma would be sufficiently seductive to make me join NEMS and take the posh-sounding job title of Senior Press and Publicity Officer which he proposed to create for me. So he said, "It's high time I took you to meet the boys. They'll be back in London again next week. How are you fixed?" Without imagining for one moment that I'd finish up working with "the boys" for almost six years between 1963 and 1968, I arranged to be at the Devonshire Arms pub where Epstein promised to bring them after they finished recording their latest radio spot at EMI House.

Undoubtedly the first useful point of contact between us was our shared Liverpool backgrounds — they had been brought up in suburbs such as Woolton, Wavertree and Dingle while I was born and raised on the opposite side of the city in Crosby. In November 1962, George was 19 years old, Paul was 20 and John had just turned 22. Ringo, also 22, was the eldest Beatle by several months and the last to join the line-up during the summer of 1962. I was 26 and had already spent seven years away from home, first at Durham University studying languages and most recently in London writing for Decca.

At 28, Brian Epstein seemed a good deal older than any of us, partly because of his in-bred air of sophistication and his immaculate grooming.

A well-polished veneer of worldliness, what he wore and how he talked commanded instant respect from The Beatles, who had virtually moved straight from classroom to bandstand without passing Go, and were still enjoying prolonged if belated adolescence. I wouldn't have pigeon-holed Epstein as a typical Liverpudlian, a Scouser, by his appearance or his BBC speaking voice. In fact the man was an aspiring actor who eventually dropped out of drama school to seek sanctuary in the security of the Epstein family's thriving retail business, whose string of shops sold a range of goods from household furniture to radio and television sets. Brian found himself a cosy niche among the management of the firm's developing chain of local record stores, North End Music Stores or NEMS. Here he showed a special flair for picking winners from the dozens of new singles that poured out from the big record companies each Friday.

I had come to the conclusion that he held a massive amount of influence over John, Paul, George and Ringo and that although both manager and group needed one another, Epstein considered himself to be very much in control of the boys' collective career. On their behalf he had a massive ego. He had assured me at the outset when he came to see me at Decca that his Beatles were destined to be as popular as Elvis Presley and he may even have believed it.

While I waited at the bar of the Devonshire Arms I noticed that several other arrivals from EMI House drew an audible ripple of recognition from the pub's other customers. One guy was even pursued through the door by a gaggle of young girls who had to be prised off him by a roadie. Nothing like this happened when The Beatles came in. Their time had yet to come.

We settled down around one of the few free tables, borrowing an extra stool to make up the number, and Epstein did a complete set of formal introductions, "This is Tony Barrow who is coming to work with us as your PR man." I thought: "He's jumping the gun a bit." I remember a lot of energetic pressing of the flesh accompanied by exaggerated Liverpudlian greetings from the four lads. "Are yer alright there, la?" "How are youse den?" And something like, "Pleased to Beatle you for the time of the year, I'm sure" from John.

My first lasting impression was of Lennon's loud voice, which turned the heads of drinkers all around the room, visibly embarrassing Epstein whose cheeks turned cherry-red.

Paul quickly launched himself into a spectacular show of generosity. Easily sliding into the role of genial party host, he whisked his way round our circle taking orders for drinks. He started with me, "Tone, you haven't got a drink." It's a Liverpudlian thing to shorten first names to the smallest possible number of syllables (ideally one) on the slightest acquaintance – The Beatles called their manager Bri or Eppy.

When the girl behind the bar had completed the drinks order and asked for the money, Paul didn't even pause to put his hand into his pocket. He simply raised it into the air high above his head to catch the attention of Brian Epstein and yelled across the intervening tables, "Bri! ... that'll be two pounds fourteen and sixpence. Plus these two packets of ciggies." Epstein walked over to the bar and paid up as if he was well used to such a scenario.

Back around the table, Paul launched into a light-hearted interrogation from which he learnt that I had never been to see The Beatles at The Cavern in Liverpool (because I was already based in London), that I knew most of the writers on the music papers (*New Musical Express, Record Mirror, Melody Maker*) because we met regularly at press receptions and concerts, and that I was really impressed with what little material I'd heard The Beatles do so far on record.

I asked Paul the stupid question that he'd hear a thousand times again as the group grew more famous and travelled around the world: "Which of you writes the words for your songs and who composes the tunes?" He explained patiently that he and John shared the composing of the music and the creation of the lyrics. "Sometimes a catchy instrumental phrase comes first and sometimes one of us puts forward a promising title-line to start off the lyrics. Occasionally one of us will complete a new number in an hour but it usually takes longer these days. We get snatches of new ideas at home in Liverpool and have to put them on the back burner while we travel down to London for a broadcast or a recording session."

Paul also chatted to me about The Beatles' several seasons at various Hamburg clubs. I was a regular reader of *Mersey Beat*, Bill Harry's specialist newspaper that covered the Liverpool music scene, and I knew that The Beatles had been making a name for themselves in Germany. Paul told me, "In the beginning we were totally unknown to the Germans and we were expected to almost literally pull people into the place where we were playing. There'd be next to nobody at any of the tables except a handful of students making a bottle of beer last half the night. We had to get people in from the doorway to sell more beer. We'd go into a big number like "Dance In The Street" and that would pull in two or three more couples. Basically it was up to us to get the

punters to buy drinks. We were trained to work almost like fairground barkers!"

At least one precedent was set during that first evening at the Devonshire Arms. Paul cadged a full pack of cigarettes from me, one by one as we talked and then the remainder as we were getting ready to leave. I reminded him that he'd just bought 40 at the bar but he muttered something about having passed those around. Throughout the next six years, particularly when we were abroad on tours, Paul "borrowed" cigarettes from me on such a regular basis and on such a scale that I began to put them on my expenses to be charged back to NEMS. Brian Epstein never disputed these items. Sometimes when Paul acquired a full pack from me he'd immediately make the benevolent gesture of offering me one back! On other occasions he'd take two from my cigarette case and hand one on to John. He was, of course, very welcome to my cigarettes and occasionally the boot was very much on the other foot. If he saw that I was running out he'd transfer several from his packet to my case. At Christmas 1963 he more than evened up the score. At his instigation, my annual present from The Beatles, hand-delivered to my desk by a uniformed footman from Asprey's, the London jewellery store, was an expensive silver table lighter which more than made up for all the filter tips he'd taken from me during the year. So, one way or another, I got more than my own back from Paul.

The Beatles and I must have approved of one another at our first meeting although I remember my wife, Corinne, describing them at first sight as "a bunch of scruffy yobs" and saying I'd be mad to leave the security of my writing job at the Decca Record Company to work with some "tin-

MEET THE BEATLES

STAR SPECIAL

Number Twelve

AN INFORMAL DATE IN WORDS & PERSONAL ALBUM PICTURES

2'6

INTRODUCED
by THEMSELVES
Written and
compiled by
TONY BARROW

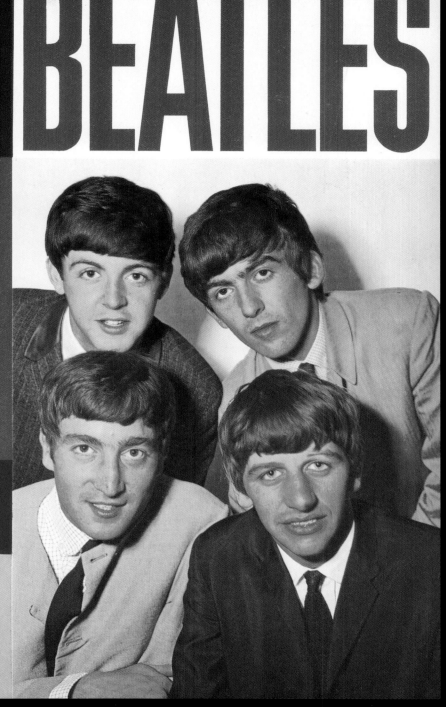

pot group from the Cavern, not even a half-decent trad jazz band".

Some weeks later Epstein treated me to a marvellous lunch at one of Wheeler's fashionable West End restaurants. Without knowing what Decca was paying me, he offered to double my current salary if I would join NEMS to establish, staff and head up his new London-based press and publicity division. Within a few months we had acquired a rather grotty one-and-a-half room first-floor office suite from Joe (Mr Piano) Henderson. Accustomed to Liverpool rental, lease and wage levels rather than the substantially higher ones that prevailed in London, Epstein was horrified at how little space we got for our money and how much I expected him to pay my freshly recruited team. For this sort of rent he wanted a sumptuously appointed Mayfair suite rather than the somewhat sleazy premises we found above a sex shop on the fringe of Covent Garden at 13, Monmouth Street, WC2.

By May 1963, having swapped Mr Piano's dim standard lamp and frayed casting couch for bright strip lighting and a lo-fi stereo system bought from NEMS in Liverpool for £33, I was ready to do Beatles business.

During the early days of the new office, The Beatles would spend whole mornings or afternoons with me giving interviews to journalists from the weekly music papers and the teenybopper magazines along with the occasional show-business writer from one of Fleet Street's national newspapers. During the course of these sessions I also fixed up phone interviews with provincial record columnists and I'd give each of The Beatles a large piece of paper with the name of the next guy they'd be talking to so that they could jump straight in with, "Hi, Gary, how are you doing?" or "Hello, Susan, you've got a sexy voice." The boys used the paper to doodle on while they did their interviews and I remember those drawings giving me my first clues to some intriguing differences between John and Paul. Paul did very realistic, meticulous images with an almost photographic quality about them, where John's drawings were all over the place, a visual nightmare in most cases. Put it this way — Paul was never the one who would draw a man with two heads or a woman with three breasts!

Because John had the loudest mouth, the myth was that John led The Beatles and wielded the most influence over Brian Epstein. The truth is that Paul was the shrewdest Beatle and the motivating force within the four. He had a genuine and sometimes obsessive ambition to attain stardom. In one of our earliest conversations he confided that he would have been willing to sign with Epstein as a solo singe–songwriter if for any reason NEMS or EMI had turned down the group as a whole. He had said to Epstein, "I hope we'll make it big as a group but I'm telling you now, Bri, I'm going to make it with or without them."

I saw Paul get his own way over and over again within the group by subtlety and suaveness. He was a cool operator. If the others were proving difficult over some press assignment I had arranged, I would encourage Paul to rally them round to the group cause, as it were. Paul would let John take the lead in situations where it suited him to do so.

John and Paul used to play the nasty and nice policemen in settling group disagreements with Epstein. When there was something contentious that the group was deeply concerned about, John would discuss it democratically with all the others

"Most of the time Paul would conduct himself in public with a visible amount of self-importance, because he knew he was about to become a very big star and he was rehearsing for it."

and then Paul would say, "Well, you know, you're right, John, something has to be done about this sooner rather than later. I think you should go and see Eppy, he's the one to get it sorted." John would be pushed into the position of spokesperson. He'd shout and storm at Epstein who would turn red-faced and might even be in tears before John had finished, but these bombastic tactics seldom won the day. John would go back to the others and have to admit defeat because he hadn't achieved anything and he'd lost the battle. At this point Paul would go to Brian with a more sympathetic, softly, softly approach, saying quietly, "Bri, there's something we need to talk about." He was wooing rather than intimidating, persuasive rather than overpowering. Epstein's defences would simply melt away as Paul looked him straight in the eye (something John was bad at) and pleaded his case. Paul would often give Eppy a hard time but all the while he'd be wearing a velvet glove. Eppy tried so hard to deal fairly with his artists and any hint of a quarrel upset him bitterly. In the case of The Beatles, Paul managed to combine elements of a business negotiator and artistic director, pressing home the group's complaints without resorting to the verbal violence that was John's speciality. At the end of the day, Paul would have won the war without further bloodshed and would be welcomed back as the homecoming hero by the other Beatles.

Paul never considered himself to be off duty. When he appeared to be operating in low profile, it was because he felt strategically moved to do so. Most of the time he would conduct himself in public with a visible amount of self-importance, because he knew he was about to become a very big star and he was rehearsing for it. When big-time fame did come for the Fab Four, Paul was ready to enjoy the glory of it.

I think Paul and I worked well together. I tended to home in on Paul for PR purposes without realising I was doing it. I found Paul by far the easiest to deal with because he really understood the value of good media exposure and knew just how to perform for the press. From the start, he seemed to know instinctively how to work the media to best advantage. When his interviewer was an attractive young female he'd flirt outrageously, using body language and the baby face to skirt around any awkward questions and make a favourable impression.

In the early days when The Beatles would pose for endless pictures, it was Paul who fetched the dullest session to life by adding appropriate bits of action. He was also the last of the four to take a final look in the mirror before letting photographers start flashing their cameras in his face. One of the first shoots I arranged for The Beatles in 1963 was a rush job with a famous showbiz photographer named Dezo Hoffmann. In as few hours as possible, we needed to get a wide range of pictures taken around the West End to make a six-page photo story entitled "A London Day In The Life Of The Beatles". As we worked, I noticed that it was Paul who animated most of Dezo's snaps by adding suitable gestures and putting on facial expressions. The first shot of our sequence showed John being coaxed out of bed and it was Paul who handed John an early-morning cup of tea. In the hotel lobby it was Paul who pointed out different suitcases to the porters as The Beatles pretended to pick out their baggage. And it was Paul again who took centre stage when the four boys were supposed to be bartering with an Italian shopkeeper in Soho.

"Paul never considered himself to be off duty."

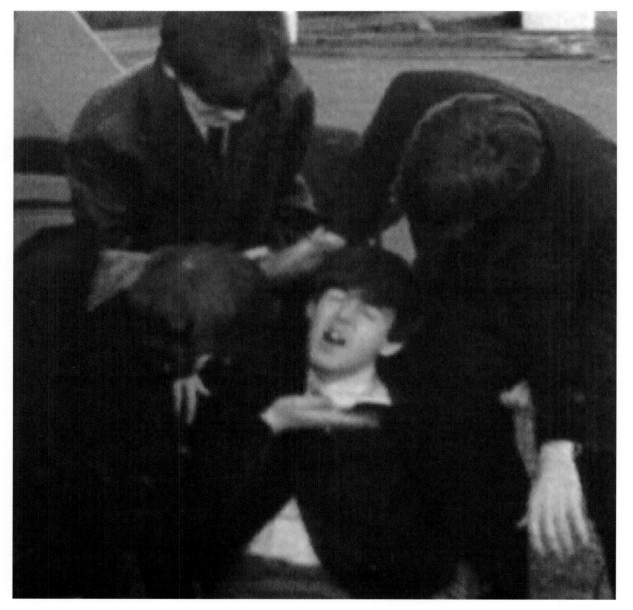

"In the early days when The Beatles would pose for endless pictures, it was Paul who fetched the dullest session to life by adding appropriate bits of action."

Dezo danced about with delight – he was used to directing every slightest gesture he wanted his pop groups to make for the camera but here was Paul doing it all for him. Paul has now passed on his knack for enlivening press shots to daughter Stella – have you noticed the way she points to some unseen object behind the camera in a lot of her pictures?

As time passed I began to realise that the main raison d'être of The Beatles was to act as a delivery vehicle for the music of Lennon and McCartney, they were the two group members who mattered most. George and Ringo were there to perform the works of Paul and John – and I think it took George some years to realise just how unlikely it was that he'd ever get one of the songs he'd written onto the A side of any Beatles single. Although Lennon and McCartney seldom sat down together in the same room with the specific intention of writing a new song, their competitive spirits communicated constantly and there was a remarkable chemistry between them when it came to composing incredibly commercial tunes and memorable lyrics. Few of their titles were truly equal collaborations; most of the time one of the two guys would bring along a 90%-completed number and the other would contribute that little extra something, maybe nothing more than a change of word here or there, which the perfect finishing touch. I found that John and Paul worked best as writers and composers when under serious pressure to meet a film premiere deadline or a pre-arranged album release date. In these circumstances Paul was the catalyst, pressing ahead with his songwriting while John just thought about his. Then quite suddenly Paul would turn up with five new songs all ready for recording and John would say, "Oh Christ, I have nothing written!" This would spur John to go away and get his side of the job done. But I felt this was part of the personal competitiveness between the two rather than for the good of the group as a whole. Call it what you will, a razor-sharp rivalry or a professional lust for supremacy, electricity almost visibly crackled between the pair and made Lennon and McCartney into an unbeatable songwriting team.

John and Paul were very much like brothers; they often shared the same hotel rooms, not only in the early days when the group was too poor to afford suites but even later on when we were touring the world and staying in five-star places. They changed around; it wasn't always Paul sharing with John, but it was convenient that they should do so if they needed to confer on the running order for their stage act or debate which new songs to bring in and which could be left out. This intensely close relationship wasn't always based on brotherly love. There was bitter jealousy between them, particularly over song-writing. John often vented his anger on Paul, condemning the simplicity of ballads such as "Yesterday". I recall a rehearsal in a Blackpool theatre auditorium where the show's cast and crew were shocked to hear John yell out obscenities about "Yesterday" which Paul was proposing to introduce for the first time. Paul had been striving for months to get "Yesterday" just right. He was justifiably proud of the end-product; it was one of his best-ever ballads. John could never have written it because he didn't have the dedication or the attention span, he'd have started it and left it half-written, whereas Paul was prepared to keep on working until the task was done.

John and Paul had some ferocious rows over A

and B sides of singles and whose song should go on the top deck of the next release – although by music business tradition the final decision on such things was supposed to lie with their record producer, George Martin, in collaboration with personal manager Brian Epstein. It was A sides that got all the radio plugs. Many ordinary record collectors and most radio DJs didn't even play B sides. Eventually something revolutionary happened when EMI started to issue double-A sides so that both Paul and John could each have a side to themselves featuring their own compositions without letting one have any sort of top billing over the other.

As their hit singles and best-selling albums piled up, so did The Beatles' workload and this forced them to leave Liverpool and live closer to their workplaces which were mainly the London recording and television studios. John, George and Ringo stayed in town for a little while, sharing luxury apartments near the West End or in Knightsbridge, but they soon became keen to set up family homes in the leafier surroundings in the Surrey stockbroker belt.

On April 18th 1963 Paul met actress Jane Asher, then 17, at the Royal Albert Hall where The Beatles were doing a BBC concert. The couple embarked upon a relationship that was to last for five years through the so-called Beatlemania years and a little beyond. At the Asher family's invitation, Paul took up residence in the garret on the top floor of their Georgian home at 57, Wimpole Street. The household included Jane's father, Richard, who was a doctor, her mother, Margaret, who spoiled Paul with her excellent cooking, Jane's brother Peter, who was to become half of the singing duo Peter & Gordon, and Jane's younger sister, Claire, an actress in the BBC

radio soap *Mrs Dale's Diary*.

The relationship was good for Paul. To him one of Jane's most appealing attributes was that she was already a celebrity and could introduce him to the fashionable London set of the early 60s, from her fellow actors to his favourite painters. Her family's well-placed society connections and her wide circle of well-respected theatrical and artistic friends suited him down to the ground. These were precisely the circles in which Paul wanted to move, fast-tracking himself through the ranks of London's contemporary scene. He loved all aspects of show business and liked to be at West End film premieres, at theatreland's glitzy opening nights and at art gallery preview parties where he could broaden his base of noteworthy friends.

Very quickly Paul and Jane began to go out together, Paul took up the Asher family's invitation to come and stay at their spacious Wimpole Street home where he was given his own top-floor rooms. In this convenient and gracious environment, Paul enjoyed a particularly fruitful period of his creative life. He was impressed by the family's very busy but perfectly organised lifestyle and he made the most of his days and nights. He and Jane could be seen attending at all the best-publicised London social events. Paul was the only Beatle to have such a thoroughly reported private life. The rest of the band tried to keep their collective professional fame well separated from their individual relationships and partners were generally kept out of the limelight whenever possible.

I was very seldom called upon to arrange twosome media interviews for any of The Beatles with their womenfolk – weddings and births were exceptions – and while Jane restricted her press work to promoting her current plays, the regular flow of press photographs of the couple out on the town kept their four-year love affair in the public eye. The fact that Paul preferred to live in town, first as a guest of the Asher family and then in his own substantial house at Cavendish Avenue, St John's Wood, had two opposing effects on his working life. On the one hand he lived a stone's throw from Abbey Road recording studios and could virtually fall into bed within minutes of finishing a late-night EMI session. On the other hand he'd often ask the others to share a nightcap with him on their way home and this tended to lead to all-night parties fuelled by a cocktail of drink and drugs. An interview that Paul gave to America's *Life* magazine about his drug-taking experiences resulted in worldwide headlines and Paul was called upon over and over again to clarify his position. At that time a careless quote or two from him could have put the public image of The Beatles in jeopardy, but I thought he handled the situation expertly, shifting some responsibility onto the press for spreading his original *Life* magazine remarks to a far wider audience. "I was asked the question and the decision I had to make was whether to tell a lie or tell the truth. The man from the newspaper is the man from the mass media and I'll keep it a personal thing if he does too. It's his responsibility for spreading whatever I say." Paul finished off by adding, "I don't think my fans are going to take drugs just because I did."

Paul's central London home-base made it easy for me to call upon him at short notice to do press business. Where the others might easily refuse point-blank to make the trip into town without a better reason than an interview, as a rule I found Paul totally co-operative and I could get him into my office within half an hour. Being close at hand didn't always make Paul punctual. Having the shortest distance to travel, he should have been the one who arrived first when the four had group appointments to keep. In reality he would often turn up last. While the roadies picked up the three rurally based Beatles in good time from Esher and Weybridge and got them wherever they had to be, Paul would be finishing his breakfast at a leisurely pace, confident that he had time to spare.

Of the four Beatles, Paul was the least damaged either physically or mentally by the battering pressures of Beatlemania during the roller-coaster touring years. When The Beatles began to play some of North America's largest outdoor stadium venues, Paul was in his element but the other three seemed to hanker for the friendly, informal environment of Liverpool's Cavern basement and the other relatively tiny city clubs and suburban dance halls on the so-called Mersey Beat circuit where the group appeared before becoming famous. At first all four found the USA awesome. George hated all aspects of air travel and the others loathed the claustrophobic conditions imposed by necessary security precautions. But Paul enjoyed most of the trappings of stardom from the airport crowds to the screaming concert audiences. When the rest of the band insisted that the touring days should finish in 1966, Paul would have criss-crossed the globe to play massive stage dates for many more years if he'd had his way — indeed he has kept up his schedules of worldwide concerts throughout the four decades since disbanding. The group's lifespan as a touring band may have stopped dead after a miserably brief few years but McCartney has stayed on the road throughout a remarkably

"Paul was the only Beatle to have such a thoroughly reported private life. The others tried to keep their collective professional fame well separated from their individual relationships and partners were generally kept out of the limelight whenever possible."

long career of 40-plus years and counting.

From the birth of Beatlemania in the second half of 1963 to the final American concert in August 1966, The Beatles were a bill-topping international concert attraction for slightly under three years. Apart from playing strings of dates in Europe, Asia and Australia, they undertook annual megatours of the USA and Canada. The first lengthy series of shows in US cities in the summer of 1964 proved to be somewhat chaotic in that travel, staging and security arrangements did not take account of and simply could not cope with the sheer magnitude and force of Beatlemania. Each city's town hall thought it could do better than everyone else but without adequate planning they all failed hopelessly at crowd control. Marauding fans were allowing to invade hotels and airports. At the group's shows they ran wild, risking all to grab a jacket or shirt button off a favourite Beatle.

Without a doubt the second tour, the one in 1965, was the best organised and The Beatles enjoyed that year's US concerts the most. Of all their gigs I would say that the date at New York's Shea Stadium that August was the greatest. Musically it was not their finest performance — no stage shows produced the most wonderful music — but as an experience Shea was totally memorable for its size and electrifying excitement.

Paul told me that the best buzz of all for him was to play for something like 50,000–60,000 people in a baseball park. He fed on the approval of his public. He did then, he does now. The second best buzz came from meeting groups of fans in controlled situations where it was possible to chat and Paul made a point of putting himself in such a position whenever possible. On tour Paul was eager to be seen as the good guy who

would promise people access to dressing rooms or even concert tickets. As often as not I was the fall guy left to deal with his unfulfilled promises. His ability to turn up the charm to order was a public relations delight, but it also put me in the awkward position of apologising to fans because I had no show tickets to dish out to them and I couldn't possibly grant backstage access to such huge numbers of people.

People assume that The Beatles' meeting with Elvis Presley was a highlight of the 1965 US tour. I have to tell you that it was almost a total disappointment — but for the fact that a pile of guitars plus Paul's piano playing helped to save the day. The Beatles wanted to meet the king of rock & roll but in the weeks beforehand they shared a growing fear that the event would turn into a media publicity circus. Paul, normally keen to make the most of any PR opportunity, told me firmly that both he and the others wanted to pull out in good time if I was planning to have a battery of press in attendance. I had to promise him that no reporters or photographers would be present and tape recorders and cameras would be banned. Not even the boys' road managers would be allowed to take any snaps. *NME* newsman Chris Hutchins was invited along but only because of his long-standing friendship with Presley's manager, Col. Tom Parker, and his involvement in bringing Parker and Epstein together to arrange the summit meeting of their clients. The Beatles argued that if Hutchins came along, I must be included too so that I could report on the evening's events to the international entourage of media people who were travelling with us throughout the tour. Brian Epstein confided to me (but not, I think, The Beatles) that a priority aim of the meeting for him would be to tempt Elvis

"McCartney has stayed on the road throughout a remarkably long career of 40-plus years and counting."

into touring the UK and Europe, possibly on a once-in-a-lifetime dream-list concert bill shared with The Beatles. Of course this did not materialise, although on the big night I saw Brian Epstein and Col Tom Parker having a lengthy pow-wow in a secluded corner of Presley's vast, circular playroom.

I didn't envy Eppy his job of negotiating terms and conditions with Parker during the days prior to the meeting. One stumbling block was the fixing of a location where the stars would come together without one side or the other losing face. Epstein tried to insist that Elvis should come over to the house The Beatles had rented for a mid-tour break at 2850 Benedict Canyon Road in the Hollywood hills. Parker won this round, forcing Epstein to agree that we'd drive over to Presley's plushy Bel Air home on Perugia Road.

The Beatles had admired Elvis Presley since the group's earliest days at home on Merseyside. Paul often discussed his teenage adoration of various American juke-box giants of the 50s but his clear favourite was Elvis. When members of the McCartney family assembled for a party they were often treated to impromptu impressions of Elvis by a hip-swivelling young Paul who would prance about the front room to the tune of "Heartbreak Hotel".

In the event the starry get-together was anti-climactic for all concerned. Maybe both the King and the Fab Four were nervous and maybe Presley was jealous of the group's massive popularity, particularly on his home ground. Either way, the five made boring small-talk for the first hour or so at Presley's place. The Beatles told their host that our chartered Lockheed Electra aircraft had caught fire on the way into Portland, Oregon, and Elvis tried to match it with his own plane-scare

anecdote. A bunch of the so-called Memphis Mafia, who travelled with Elvis as his minders and gofers, saw to it that Bourbon, Scotch, Tequila and other ice-breakers flowed freely but the party failed to warm up. Finally, Elvis said to Paul something like, "Didn't you guys show up here to jam?" With that he called on his henchmen to bring on some guitars and he turned down the sound on the television for the first time since our arrival. Now the proceedings came to life big-time. They all sat round on this crescent-shaped sofa and the sparkle that had been missing from their verbal conversation was now replaced by a colourful exchange of musical conversation. They could converse in music where they had been lost for words without their instruments. Paul played the piano at one point and Ringo tapped out a backbeat on the woodwork, which much amused Paul, "Look! They've given Ringo a pair of drum sticks but no kit to play!" Tongue planted firmly in his cheek, Paul showed Elvis some guitar chords and told him, "We'll make a decent player of you and then Brian Epstein can give you a whole new career!" Paul nutshelled his own feelings afterwards. "I sort of liked the guy. We tried to persuade him to make some new records like the old sound that made him famous. If he does, I'll be down at the record store with my shilling in my hand!"

It is another myth that The Beatles held mass orgies and sex parties all night and every night whenever they were abroad and separated from their usual partners. One tour I did not go on was their trip to Australia in 1964 so I asked them about it when they returned home. Instead of relaying tantalising tales of womanising, Paul told me, "I read just about every James Bond book ever published. I started on the long-haul flight and the idea turned into a craze that spread through the group. By the end of the tour we were talking about little else other than James Bond and what he'd been up to in the most recent book we'd read." Of course there was plenty of partying, particularly on the longer US tours, but there were also many nights when the boys put up their Do Not Disturb signs and behind closed doors indulged in nothing more exciting than playing a few board games or word games among themselves. Under-age teenage fans used to fantasise to their friends about non-existent bedroom sessions with the boys but the truth is that when The Beatles did entertain women in their hotel suites after hours they were adults rather than youthful fans and they were as often as not old friends from the music business.

In 1965 The Beatles enjoyed themselves on tour; it was unarguably their happiest year on the road. They were playing at being superstars and finding the game to be good fun. It was all smiles and deep joy. In 1966 they had grown weary of the whole idea of travelling from continent to continent, stadium to stadium, in uncomfortable conditions. The fun had gone, only the punishment of the gruelling tour schedules remained. At the beginning of the summer, before their US dates, The Beatles had been to Germany, Japan and the Philippines. After we moved on from the nostalgic German leg of the tour, a series of traumatic incidents tore the smiles from the faces of John, Paul, George and Ringo and robbed them of their self-confidence. In Tokyo a faction of student extremists had threatened to assassinate the group if they dared to play any of their five scheduled concerts at the Budokan, a venue reserved for serious sporting fixtures and hitherto never rented out for rock or pop shows. In Manila

President Ferdinand Marcos gave the group a hard time for not turning up to a high-society luncheon in their honour. As we left the country, a carefully orchestrated mob of armed thugs physically and verbally intimidated our party as we passed through the airport to our KLM aircraft.

Finally, to complete a trilogy of disasters, John's statement that The Beatles had become more popular than Jesus stirred up hatred, particularly among zealots in America's so-called Southern Bible Belt, giving publicity-seeking local DJs the chance to organise bonfires at which The Beatles' albums were ceremonially burned. Worse still, Bible Belt extremists terrorised The Beatles by promising to take John's life when the tour took us down into the Southern states. All these factors contributed to a grim year of fear, which took its toll on The Beatles and put them off touring. Quite apart from the death threats which were worrying enough, the boys felt they had other good reasons to quit touring and stick to making records in future. Artistically, musically, the concerts no longer held any appeal for the boys, George in particular, because the stuff they played could not be heard above the constant screaming of the fans. On August 26, 1966, in a suite on the first floor of Capitol Tower, the Hollywood headquarters of their US record company, The Beatles gave their last major press conference as a touring band and this was the last occasion that I organised and moderated such an event for them. Most noticeable throughout the 20-minute conference was the group's change in attitude to the media. At the Capitol Tower event they treated an audience of prestigious international journalists with indifference bordering on contempt. Only Paul made any attempt to offer more than monosyllabic answers,

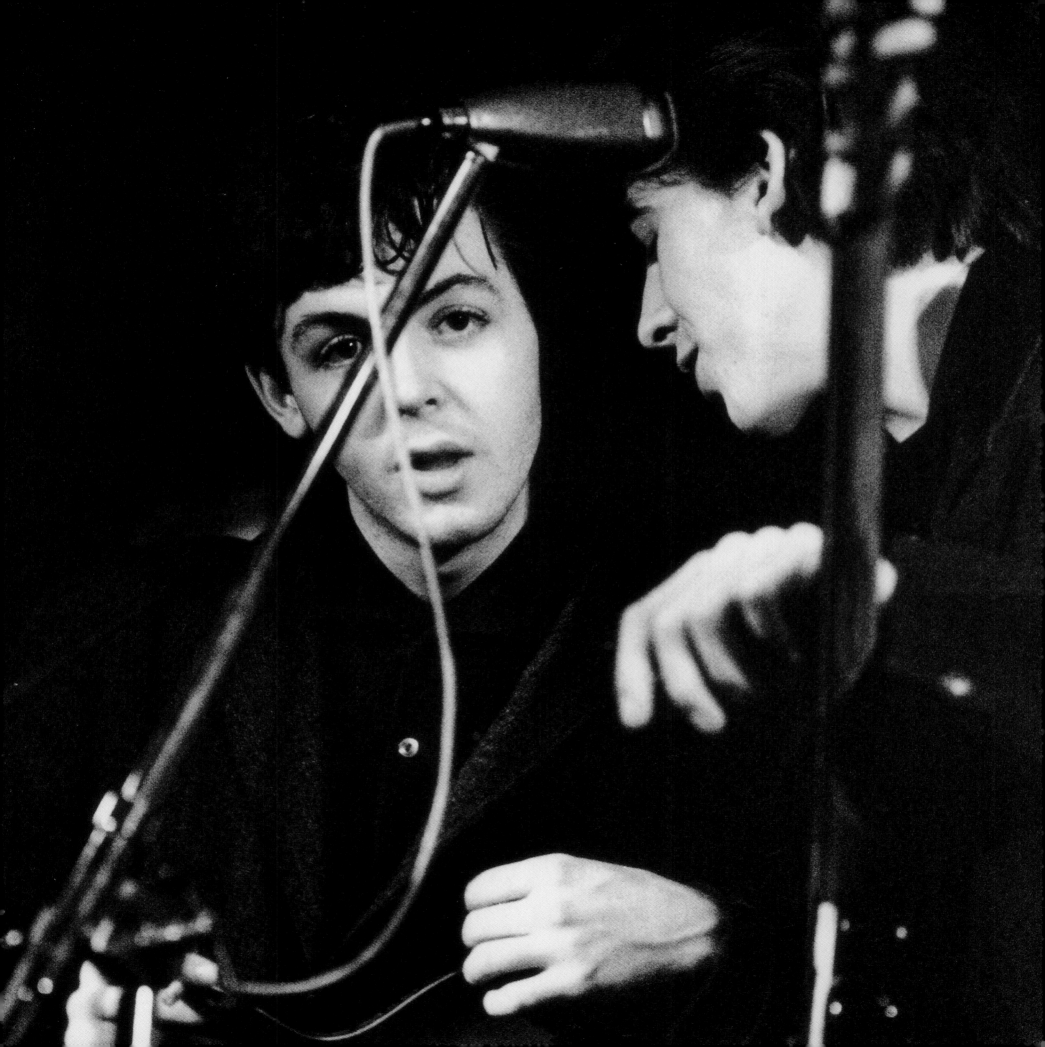

trying as always to save the day.

Question: "A recent article in *Time* magazine referred to "Day Tripper" as being about a prostitute and "Norwegian Wood" as being about a lesbian. What was your intent when you wrote them?

Paul: "We were just trying to write songs about prostitutes and lesbians, that's all."

Several days later The Beatles gave their final concert at San Francisco's Candlestick Park, a romantic name for an unpretty baseball park in need of renovation. On the way to the gig, Paul said, "Make me a recording of tonight's concert will you?" Neither he nor any of the others had ever asked me to make a private souvenir recording of previous concerts, even to mark the end of each major tour. Was this just a sentimental end-of-term impulse on Paul's part or did he realise that this would be the last full-blown concert The Beatles would ever give? As the stands filled up around the park I moved around the tall banks of speakers on the field, deciding on the best position for my Philips portable tape recorder and Beyer microphone. While The Beatles tuned up on stage I switched on the recorder and held my microphone high in the air in the general direction of a nearby bank of speakers. "Yesterday" came out best — this was the closest the Candlestick Park audience came to actually listening rather than screaming their heads off. In his next bit of patter, Paul remarked that there was a nasty wind sweeping across the park and made his own indirect reference to the fact that this was the last show of the tour. Before introducing Ringo's "I Want To Be Your Man", Paul said, "It's a bit chilly. We'd like to do this next number now which is a request for all the wonderful backroom boys on this tour ..."

Years later I compared my Candlestick Park audio cassette recording with a video of the Fab Four's 1963 concert in Washington and realised that apart from minor changes such as his comment on the weather, Paul used the same words to announce each of their songs, although three years passed between these two shows.

I have a bitter-sweet postscript to this Candlestick Park anecdote. Thirty years on, in the mid-90s, I was thinking about putting my original copy of the Candlestick Park cassette up for sale by auction, having re-recorded the concert material onto a fresh tape for my own use. Before going any further, I checked with Paul to give him first option on acquiring the original if he felt it had any sentimental value. It turned out that he'd lost his copy and wanted me to make a fresh one for him, which I said I'd be happy to do. Then came a follow-up call from his office saying, "Paul wants to know how much you're going to charge him for copying the cassette." I said that of course there'd be no charge, adding facetiously that he could pay me for the blank tape and postage costs if he liked! But it saddened me to think that Paul quite expected an old friend to charge him some sort of fee for such a simple favour and I wondered just how many self-styled buddies, pals and mates of his were/are in the habit of ripping him off as a matter of course in similar circumstances. I didn't sell the original cassette after all and it is now stored safely in a bank deposit box.

Within days of Brian Epstein's tragically premature death at the end of August 1967, scarcely waiting for the funeral to take place, Paul called an emergency strategy meeting of The Beatles to take place at his London house in Cavendish Avenue, St John's Wood. Some of the

group's closest aides were shocked by the speed of his action and accused him of being callous and uncaring. Paul deliberately asked me to arrive before the group so that he could put me in the picture. In gist, his plan was to go ahead at once with the making of his zany musical film, *Magical Mystery Tour*, and he wanted to put together an informal shooting schedule as soon as possible. His chief reason for rushing things was his concern that John, George and Ringo might turn to their newly discovered guru, Transcendental Meditation practitioner Maharishi Mahesh Yogi, whose recent series of lectures in London and in Bangor, North Wales, had been attended by a cross-section of fashionable celebrities including members of the Fab Four. It was during the August Bank Holiday weekend in Bangor with the Maharishi that The Beatles had been told of Epstein's death and in their shock and grief he had been the first person they looked to for advice. Not the greatest fan of Transcendental Meditation, Paul saw how vulnerable his colleagues were in the wake of their manager's demise. He told me solemnly, "If the Maharishi takes The Beatles back to India with him on one of his extended meditation courses, I doubt if the four of us will ever come back together again as a working band."

Having completed their *Sgt Pepper* album the boys would have found themselves without a new project to tackle had it not been for Paul's *Magical Mystery Tour*. Epstein's death complicated the issue, raising questions about the future that nobody felt capable of answering. Putting himself and the others to work right away on a such an ambitious adventure as the making of *Magical Mystery Tour* was Paul's way of trying to hold The Beatles together, getting them

thoroughly involved before the moment passed. He also had a second, more basic motive. Paul hoped to mastermind a new phase of the group's career in movies, putting himself in control as The Beatles' film producer. After that, who knew? Hollywood?

While we waited for the remaining group members, Paul outlined his ideas, recalling how we all went off for family outings to Blackpool lights in coaches when we were kids "with a crate of ale stashed in the boot for the sing-song on the way back." He went on, "We called them charabanc trips, didn't we, and sometimes we were taken to mystery destinations. So we'll hire an old bus and drive off somewhere, probably the West Country, and *Magical Mystery Tour* will be a film record of all the fun we can have along the way." Paul had created four quirky and comic central characters for The Beatles to play and plenty of supporting roles for which he'd select suitable-looking professional actors and actresses from the pages of the Spotlight theatrical directory. All four Beatles would be asked to contribute two or three comedy sequences, making them as farcical as they liked. This would divide responsibility equally among everybody and create a wide range of comedic styles.

I had my doubts about how John, George and Ringo would react. In the event they rallied round and played Paul's game enthusiastically. It didn't seem to matter that there was no script for the film, no proper shooting schedule and no professional production crew booked. None of us in the group's circle of professional aides and advisers had the slightest experience of film-making but, like the boys themselves, we allowed ourselves to be pumped up by Paul's very powerful enthusiasm and we all went to work

Following page:
"Paul's reason for rushing things was his concern that the other Beatles might turn to their newly discovered guru, Transcendental Meditation practitioner Maharishi Mahesh Yogi, whose recent series of lectures in London and in Bangor, North Wales, had been attended by a cross-section of fashionable celebrities including the Fab Four."

brimming with passionate optimism.

Intended in Paul's mind for international theatrical release, *Magical Mystery Tour* didn't make it into the cinemas but finished up on television at Christmas 1967 and was panned by the critics. To get a thumbs-down signal from the press was a rare experience for The Beatles and one that put paid to Paul's ambitions as a movie producer. But the venture had kept the group together as a working band, according to Paul's plan, and The Beatles simply licked their wounds, took off belatedly for India and the Maharishi's next meditation course and then went back to Abbey Road to make some new records. Paul tried hard to conceal his bitter disappointment but there was long-term damage done to his professional ego.

I think maybe the way in which Paul took control of *Magical Mystery Tour* left a bad taste in the mouths of John, George and Ringo. Everyone had agreed that Brian Epstein could not and should not be replaced and that the group would look after its own management affairs in the wake of his death. Despite this, Paul had proved how easy it was to assume a position of supremacy in what was supposed to be a democratic unit.

There was a positive side to *Magical Mystery Tour*. The soundtrack threw up a small collection of excellent new songs, which were recorded on a pair of EP (extended play) discs, packaged together with a colourful little booklet containing a strip-cartoon version of the film's story. Paul handed me the job of compiling and editing the cartoon booklet, saying he'd like the pages to look "a bit like Rupert Bear". I hired a caricature artist who had worked with The Beatles before and I set to work on writing the words to go beneath each of the cartoon pictures. I was pleasantly surprised at the amount of his own time and interest Paul poured into the putting together of the booklet, dropping into the Soho art studio we were using quite regularly to catch up on progress and make suggestions. He would play around with literally one or two words for ages before satisfying himself that a single sentence sounded precisely the way he wanted.

Had *Magical Mystery Tour* been a unanimous success with press and public alike, the others might have turned a blind eye to what they considered to be Paul's heavy-handed manipulations and manoeuvres. But the kindest critical comment had been that the comedy content of the film was "ahead of its time", which translated as "too way out for us". In these circumstances every slightest new policy proposal from Paul from this point on was treated with suspicion.

By this time Paul had met and was falling for New York showbiz photographer Linda Eastman. He had been on the brink of marrying Jane after what the public saw as a beautiful five-year fairy-tale romance. In June 1968, when Paul was best man at the wedding of his younger brother, Mike, there was no visible split in their relationship, even in the relative privacy of the McCartney family home on Merseyside. A smiling Jane was to be seen in the wedding pictures snuggling up to Paul, and at the evening reception afterwards I remember noticing how right they looked together. In my mind I was speculating about how few weeks it might be before I would call the media with news of another McCartney marriage.

Meanwhile an ambitious American fan named Francie Schwartz had temporarily come onto the scene. Francie came to London and called at The Beatles' new Apple offices with a film project for which she wanted Paul to write some songs. Catching Paul's eye in the office entrance hall, she grabbed the chance of putting her case to him in person. Paul responded well without making any firm promises on the film idea but, meanwhile, there seemed to be a more personal interest. Indeed, he fixed her up with a temporary job as a press office assistant at Apple and went on to take the unusual step of introducing Francie to the whole group in the Abbey Road studios when he invited her to visit The Beatles' latest batch of recording sessions for the *White Album*. At the time I didn't see the full significance of this move although it was almost unheard of for a member of The Beatles to invite any outsider into the carefully guarded sanctuary that was their workplace. I thought to myself, "It's a tit-for-tat thing. Paul sees that John has brought Yoko in, so he's brought this Francie girl. Love all." Like Yoko, Francie was a totally unknown quantity so far as the other Beatles were concerned. All they knew was that she was an American, a bit pushy, and not Paul's type at all.

Jane was soon to make as dignified an exit as possible, and soon after spoke of the end of her engagement to Paul on DJ Simon Dee's BBC TV show, broadcast on July 20. She told one reporter, "Perhaps we'll be childhood sweethearts who meet up again and get married when we're about 70." In October Linda moved in at Cavendish Avenue with her daughter, Heather, and the couple were together for the next 30 years until Linda's death in April 1998.

When John, Paul, George and Ringo concentrated all their business affairs under the umbrella of their self-management company, Apple Corps, my job as The Beatles' personal PR man came to a natural end. Neither Paul nor the others wanted to do any more interviews about The Beatles although they would agree to talk about Apple projects — in Paul's case this meant, for example, the launch of his Welsh singing protégé, Mary Hopkin. I never wanted to be part of the Apple set-up and left NEMS Enterprises a year after Epstein's death to set up my own independent showbiz PR firm.

"When The Beatles concentrated their business affairs under Apple Corps, my job as their personal PR came to an end"

Long after the break-up of The Beatles, Paul came back to me when his and Linda's *Ram* album was ready for release in 1972. Our brief professional reunion failed to work out, not because of any issue with the album, but because Paul wanted to get me involved in a strange remote-control PR campaign for *Ram*. I was to play his LP tracks to journalists and DJs at my new company's London offices while he stayed on his Scottish farm some 538 miles away! I felt the least he could have done to support the campaign would have been to face the media in person and talk about the music. "Can't you make it all up like we used to do?" he asked.

today...

In the opening weeks of 2004, Sir Paul McCartney looked over the new year's international album charts with a special sense of pleasure. Holding its place among the best-sellers around the globe was The Beatles, *Let It Be ...Naked*, a significantly re-worked version of the 1970 album with all traces of "guest" producer Phil Spector's input removed. McCartney had always disliked the Spector version from the outset and now, finally, it had been exorcised.

The original version of *Let It Be* was at the epicentre of a clash between Paul and John Lennon, although their quarrels were about much more than the making of an album: they were about the group's entire future and whether or not the Fab Four could go on working together. It was the album's misfortune to become mixed up in the preliminary brawl that led up to the final litigious disbanding of The Beatles in 1970. In general all four members of the group were un-happy about aspects of *Let It Be* and didn't want it to be put out without further work being done to improve most of the tracks. At any other point in the band's history, creative/artistic disagreement among the group over the production of the album would have been solved in the usual democratic way but by May 1970, Paul was no longer on speaking terms with John, George and Ringo. The three had put their faith in American entrepreneur Allan Klein, unilaterally handing him control of The Beatles' management without proper discussion with Paul, who was dead against using Klein. The waters were made muddier by the fact that Paul's new bride, Linda, belonged to a family of distinguished New York lawyers in whom Paul was inclined to pin his faith. To make matters worse Klein had recommended Phil Spector as the best person to

re-brand *Let It Be* with his own distinctive style of production, a move that infuriated Paul, who felt that any repolishing of the recordings should be done within the group, with or without the collaboration of The Beatles' long-term record producer, George Martin. Seemingly by deliberate conspiracy, the other Beatles prevented Paul from hearing much of the Spector version of the album until it was too late to make new changes. Mean-while, unaware of the wide scope of Spector's doctoring brief, Paul went ahead with putting finishing touches to his own hastily assembled and self-produced album, *McCartney*, which Apple issued in April 1970, three weeks prior to *Let It Be*. Paul saw this clash of dates as sheer victimisation, quite rightly claiming that the public vote would be split and both albums would suffer from reduced sales as a result of the two rival albums hitting the shops almost simultaneously. When he finally got to hear *Let It Be*, Paul was particularly offended by Spector's "enhancement" of "The Long And Winding Road", complaining loudly and bitterly to those in his immediate circle that he would never have authorised the addition of horns, strings and a heavenly choir. For this to have happened at a point of no return proved to Paul that he had lost his dominant share in the artistic control of The Beatles' musical output. John Lennon belittled Paul's complaints, saying, "Paul should be grateful to Phil for salvaging something from the most miserable recording sessions that ever existed, tapes than none of us wanted to even listen to ever again." Meanwhile, the critics were not kind to the George Martin–Glynn Johns–Phil Spector production collaboration. Even Liverpudlian journalist Alan Smith, a long-standing buddy, pal and mate of all four boys, wrote in the music industry bible, *New Musical Express*, that *Let It Be* was a "cardboard tombstone" that represented "a cheapskate epitaph, a sad and tatty end" to the group's recording career.

For the next 33 years, Paul nursed his deep grievances over *Let It Be* and looked forward to a time when he might arrange a complete make-over job to put the album back to the way it was before Spector's intervention. Then, a year into the 21st century, he was pleasantly surprised to note the phenomenal sales of over 20 million copies achieved by Apple's latest compilation, *1*, an album that collected together 27 of the Fab Four's chart-topping singles from the 60s. This became the biggest-selling CD of the year and topped the charts for 16 weeks in markets around the world. One financial newspaper called it an "£18m windfall" for Apple and each of the surviving ex-Beatles. Paul himself said it was great that The Beatles' hits held up and sounded so good all these years later. "I am very chuffed with it being No 1 in more countries than any other album ever, 34 countries," he told reporters outside his London home. He added that at the time of their greatest popularity as a working band in the middle 60s, The Beatles had never seen anything more than a short-term future for themselves. He confessed candidly, "We thought we would be finished after about 10 years." What Paul saw as particularly fantastic was the large number of young people who were getting into the group's music for the first time, 30 years on at the turn of the century. He was equally gratified to see the huge success of *Wingspan*, a 2-CD compilation of tracks recorded by his Wings band after the break-up of The Beatles. To him this was an encouraging indication of ongoing public interest, not only in the work of the Fab Four but also material he recorded in his own

right during the early part of his solo career. And undoubtedly it was the success of the *1* compilation that persuaded Paul to put greater emphasis on songs from the Beatlemania era when he came to compile his latest stage act for the first McCartney concert tours of the 21st century in 2002.

When the unadorned *Let It Be …Naked* went on sale in November 2003, the event put The Beatles back on the front cover of *New Musical Express* where they had featured so frequently during their short lifespan as a working band in the 60s. Veteran journalist and author Ray Connolly, who began his long and diverse career as a sub-editor on the *Liverpool Echo*, wrote in the *Daily Mail*: "Paul has finally won. The digital sound is wonderful and the group sound as close as ever."

A new era of Paul's life opened in the spring of 1999 when he met Heather Mills. Their paths crossed at the *Daily Mirror's* Pride Of Britain charity awards show and, according to Paul's memory of the occasion, the WOW! factor kicked in for him at first sight of this "very beautiful, fine-looking woman".

Having been struck by her stunning looks, Paul found himself equally impressed when he heard her speak to her fellow charity workers and hand out an award to a young girl who had lost her arms and legs through meningitis. In a subsequent interview with *Hello!* magazine Paul recalled what happened next: "I found out her phone number – like you do – and rang her and suggested we should talk about some charity stuff and that I liked what she was doing."

On his first attempt to reach Heather, Paul had to content himself with leaving a message on her answering machine – Heather was away on a trip to Cambodia. Paul said, "We had three or four

meetings, all prim and proper. She came to the office to talk about the charity and I realised I fancied her. I did fancy her from the start but I was playing it cool." Heather revealed later that Paul's first present to her was a £150,000 donation to her Health Trust charity fund to improve conditions at a clinic in Sierra Leone. Talking to *Prima* magazine, Heather said that the relationship grew in slow-burn mode. "It evolved very slowly. I was properly dated and properly wooed. I had flowers sent to me; I was sung to on the phone, sung to while I was making dinner. I thought: 'This is unbelievable! This is what people dream of!' I'm a total romantic."

The 26-year age gap between the couple — when their relationship began to develop she was 32 and he was 58 — was an irrelevance. Heather told *Prima*, "He's energising — like a kind of Peter Pan character. When you see him walking down the street, he literally skips, just like a little boy. In many ways, he's definitely the youngest guy I've ever been out with. Psychologically, I feel on an equal level with Paul. There are a million reasons why I love him, but the main one is that I'm with someone who is totally secure in who he is and doesn't resent my work. We're together seven days a week. We sit down and go through our diaries together each month, and we won't do anything if it takes us away from each other."

In the summer of 2001, during a candlelit dinner, Paul went down on one knee in the old-fashioned way and formally proposed to Heather, presenting her with a large Indian ring of sapphire and diamonds set in white gold. Days later a formal press release from MPL, McCartney's production company headquarters in London's Soho Square said: "Paul McCartney and Heather Mills are pleased to announce their engagement. The couple are looking forward to being married some time next year." Paul told reporters that he and Heather were very much in love. "I'm still in shock but I'm over the moon. I was just a little nervous when I proposed, but I managed. We've had a good reception from friends, relatives and the media."

By planning to marry for a second time Paul was following in the footsteps of his father, Jim McCartney. Like Paul, Jim had lost his first wife, Mary, to breast cancer — she died in October 1956 when Paul was just 14 years old. At first Jim made up his mind to bring up his two teenage sons, Paul and his younger brother Michael, on his own. The extended McCartney family, mostly based on Merseyside, lent a helping hand. Then, after waiting some eight years until both boys had grown up, Jim remarried in 1964, this time to widow Angie Williams, who had a five-year-old daughter named Ruth. Hearing the news of Paul's engagement to Heather, Ruth, now 42 and living in California, said she was well-pleased to know that Paul would not spend the rest of his years alone. She added, "Although I'm sure he will never truly recover from the loss of his 30-year soulmate, Linda, at least he has someone with whom to share the memories of the past and the dreams of the future."

Not long after the wedding Heather described her marriage so far as "really happy" and "incredibly passionate". "It's intense all the time, and we love each other's company. Our favourite thing is to stay home. I cook a meal — Indian or Thai or Italian — and he dances around the room like Fred Astaire." But she also spoke of "a lot of unhappiness" that apparently came as unwanted baggage with her marriage. Asked about this by a journalist from music magazine *Mojo*, Paul

"Paul increased the nostalgia count tenfold on a couple of occasions by introducing instruments with special personal significance – for 'Something' it was a ukulele which he told his audience George had given him."

explained, "I think the shock for Heather was that she'd been 'great model who overcomes accident and now does a lot of work for charity and disabled people'. The minute she married me, it was 'who does she think she is?' It's really quite unfair, but she's a sitting target. I think it did give her a lot of grief. The same thing happened in the early days with Linda, but as Parky [British TV talk show host Michael Parkinson] said on his show, it comes with the territory."

Having endured two ectopic pregnancies during her previous marriage, Heather believed she needed a generous measure of good fortune if she was to conceive successfully with Paul. Her fears were put to rest when she became pregnant at the beginning of 2003, giving birth to a baby daughter weighing just 7lbs in October. Delivered by emergency caesarian operation some 17 days ahead of the predicted date, the ecstatic parents named their "little bundle of joy" Beatrice after Heather's mother and Milly after one of Paul's aunts, the younger sister of Paul's father, Jim, who cared for him and to whom he became specially close following his mother's death. "She's a little beauty and we couldn't be prouder" announced Paul. This was Heather's first child and Paul's fourth, the others being adopted step-daughter Heather from Linda's first marriage, now a professional potter, Mary, a photographer and animal-rights campaigner, Stella, a famous fashion designer, and the youngest, James, a musician and architect who has continued to live with Paul and Heather at the McCartney farmhouse home in Sussex, where our story began.

Paul McCartney's most recent series of concerts had taken place way back in 1993 and the nine-year gap without any new string of live dates in his engagement diary led to speculation

that he might not be planning to do any more stage shows now that he was approaching his 60th birthday. But at the end of January 2002 he announced a major new 19-date American tour entitled Driving USA to open in Oakland, California, on April 1st, and culminating on May 18th with a final show at Florida's Fort Lauderdale National Center.

Inevitably additional dates were added to extend the tour in the wake of speedy venue box-office sell-outs across North America, and Paul said he was "chuffed to be asked to stay longer on the road". Describing Driving USA as "one of the rock & roll events of all time" the tour promoters declared, "Maccamania is here again. We knew the gigs would be hot but this demand is boiling!" With seats priced at up to 250 dollars each, 75,000 tickets for the first five concerts sold out by telephone and internet within 30 minutes. Asked by a reporter from the *Chicago Tribune* to comment on ticket prices, Paul replied, "This ain't Streisand. We're not trying to take advantage. I always ask my promoter how much Madonna charges. And what does Elton charge? And what does U2 charge? They always give me a ballpark figure and that's what I charge."

On the tour's first night at Oakland, a suburb of San Francisco, emotional moments that brought both Paul and many of his audience close to tears ranged from his performance of "My Love.", originally dedicated to Linda when Paul sang it with Wings in 1973, to the song "Here Today" from the 1982 album *Tug Of War*, which Paul dedicated to his "dear friend John", and the Harrison composition "Something From Abbey Road", played as a moving tribute to George.

One of the earliest concerts of the series was on April 6th in a 15,000-seater arena, part of the

Paul McCartney with his trademark Beatle bass on the Driving USA tour.

MGM Grand hotel and casino complex in Las Vegas. US news sources reported that Paul's four-million-dollar fee made him the highest-paid British entertainer in Las Vegas history.

His initial tour announcement had promised a tendency towards the nostalgic and his list of songs confirmed it, opening with "Hello Goodbye" and including such titles as "All My Loving", "We Can Work It Out", "The Fool On The Hill", "Eleanor Rigby", "Here There And Everywhere" and "Can't Buy Me Love", which Paul likes to refer to as "Cor Blimey Luv!", during rehearsals. He closed with "Let It Be" and "Hey Jude", returning to do five more songs from the 60s including "The Long And Winding Road", "Yesterday" and "Sgt Pepper's Lonely Hearts Club Band". The rest of Paul's lengthy stamina-testing show relied on some well-chosen songs from his latest album, *Driving Rain*. He was on stage at each of the Driving USA shows for almost five times as long as an average Beatles concert from the mid-60s!

Paul presented relatives of people who lost their lives in the Pentagon terrorist attack on September 11th 2001 with hundreds of guest tickets for his show at Washington's MCI Center on April 23rd and he auctioned a dozen VIP seats at the second of his two Madison Square Garden gigs on April 27th to aid the Cheering For Children campaign. At the New York venue Paul accepted the honorary badge of a NYPD detective in recognition for his unstinting charitable work in the wake of the 9/11 disaster. Paul added "Mull Of Kintyre" to his set for a show at Toronto's 15,000-seater Air Canada Centre, where tickets had sold out within half an hour of becoming available, enlisting fourteen pipers and eight drummers from Peel Regional Police Pipe Band to

accompany him on stage – the band had appeared with him for the same purpose in the 1993 New World Tour concert. A special acoustic section of the show where the rest of the band were sent off for a short break became a tour highlight, ushered in with Paul's plaintive interpretation of "Blackbird" for which he played an acoustic guitar. He increased the nostalgia count tenfold on a couple of occasions by introducing instruments with special personal significance – for "Something" it was a ukulele which he told his audience George had given him, and for "Yesterday" it was the very same acoustic guitar he'd used some 38 years earlier on the *Ed Sullivan Show!*

June 2002 must stand as a memorable month for Paul in both public and private sectors of his busy life. On June 3rd he headed the star-stacked cast of the Party At The Palace, a concert staged in Her Majesty's back garden at Buckingham Palace to mark her Golden Jubilee. At the end of a marathon show that had been beamed around the planet to an estimated 200 million viewers Paul told the crowd of 12,000 guests that he'd asked the Queen if "we'll be doing this again next year" and she'd replied, "Not in my garden!" Afterwards Paul said, "It was just fantastic. It's been a really buzzy day. When I was singing I just suddenly realised there were people in the Mall, all over Britain and all over the world listening. That's a big audience!" Later in the month he married Heather, celebrated his 60th birthday and honeymooned with his new bride on the tiny island of Cousine in the Seychelles.

BBC World Service broadcast a birthday interview in which he talked candidly about the death of his first wife and the blossoming of a new romance with Heather. He said it took him a long time to come to terms with Linda's passing. "I had a year of great difficulty when I cried a lot and looked at what my feelings were. After about 15 months I began to realise that life goes on and you have to pick up the pieces." Bringing the interview up to date Paul spoke of current concerts and song-writing, assessing the relative priorities of each in his foreseeable future. "Here we are at a new beginning and the sun is shining. I don't see any point in standing still. If I go on a tour I will have to sing 'Yesterday' for the umpteenth time and I don't mind that. But if I couldn't write anything new I would find that a problem. There is always a better song to be written." Ruling out retirement at least as any kind of near-to-middle-distant option, Paul said that whenever he felt on the brink of packing it all in, he did one gig, loved it and decided to have some more.

A second stage of Paul's 2002 tour, this one entitled Back In The USA, consisted of an additional series of autumn concerts in 23 cities, opening on September 12th at Milwaukee's Bradley Center and running through until October 29th when the final show took place at the America West Arena in Phoenix. There were some return dates to places already covered in the spring, including the MGM Grand in Las Vegas, but this new batch of gigs also took the show to a wide spread of territories not previously visited. Paul concluded each of his appearances with the promise, "See you next time!", putting paid to rumours that these might well be his farewell dates in North America. Nor was Paul's touring year over — during the first half of November the show moved on first to Mexico City and then to Tokyo and Osaka in Japan.

Reportedly the world's highest-earning celebrity of 2002 with an estimated income of £120m, more than half of which came from US touring and album sales, Paul does not have to continually criss-cross the globe and undertake physically draining concert tours in order to live securely and comfortable for the rest of his life at his chosen level of luxury. His drive is based on instinctive showmanship, not basic necessity. After a sparkling solo career that has already spanned four decades, Paul admits "It's what I do. You don't work music, you play music and I hope to be singing and playing when I'm 90 years old. I always thought I would live until about 90 and that estimate is going up. In the end I will probably be wheeled up on stage to sing 'Yesterday'."

On November 29th, eleven days after his final Japanese concert, Paul took part in the Concert For George at London's Royal Albert Hall, with profits donated to the Material World Charitable Foundation. Taking part were a host of impressive and relevant names including Ravi Shankar's daughter, Anoushka, George Harrison's son, Dhani, Eric Clapton, Jeff Lynne, Joe Brown, Billy Preston, Tom Petty and members of *Monty Python's Flying Circus*. This tribute marked the first anniversary of George's death and devoted a first half to Indian music. Although he did not play, Ravi Shankar watched from the wings with George's widow, Olivia. In the second half, Ringo Starr, the only other surviving member of the Fab Four, joined Paul on stage, turning this into a particularly noteworthy event for fans of The Beatles. Ringo brought Paul on, introducing him as "another of my friends", and Paul did "For You Blue", "Something" and 'All Things Must Pass".

Paul's Tour schedule for 2003 took him from Moscow to Merseyside but the year began with one of the most extraordinary gigs of his solo career – a private concert for some 150 privileged guests at the Ranch Blues Club in San Diego. The performance was a one-million-dollar surprise 50th birthday present from financier Ralph Whitworth to his wife, Wendy, a television executive producer with CNN. Paul sang and played with his band for some 90 minutes, presenting Wendy Whitworth with 50 birthday roses before dancing with her. At the end Paul said, "Normally, I don't do this sort of gig but I was chuffed to do it because it was a win-win show. Ralph got to be a great husband for organising the surprise, his wife got a rocking party, I got to rehearse the band for the [European] tour and, most importantly, Adopt-A-Minefield gets one million dollars. It was a very human evening and we all had a fabulous time."

Donating his fee to charity on this occasion was nothing new for Paul and this aspect of his solo career clearly played some part in his selection for a knighthood. Over the years he has given various record royalty and appearance revenues to a range of good causes, particularly some associated with animal welfare, including those supported by both his first wife, Linda, and his second wife, Heather. There is also his personal crusade to revive his old school and turn it into the Liverpool Institute of Performing Arts.

At Christmas in 2001, Paul wrote to Britain's prime minister, Tony Blair, asking him to take action on the Labour government's proposed ban on hunting with dogs. His letter was also signed by his daughters, Stella and Mary, by other McCartney family members and by a number of other influential supporters. Dating the letter December 26th, Paul wrote: "All around the country today people on horseback will be marking Boxing Day by following packs of hounds chasing and savaging hundreds of wild animals in the name of sport. We want to live in a country where it is illegal to inflict pain and suffering by hunting wild animals with dogs, an activity that we, along with most British people, believe is cruel, unnecessary, unacceptable and outdated. Your government promised to give the House of Commons an early opportunity to express its view, to have a free vote and to enable parliament to reach a conclusion on this issue. The time to do this has come."

In January 2002 Paul received a Lifetime Achievement Award from Amnesty International at a ceremony in New York for helping to "educate the public about human rights, raise awareness on a variety of critical social issues" and in recognition of his support for animal rights, famine relief and landmine bans. Royalties from Heather's autobiography, originally called *Out On A Limb* and later re-titled *A Single Step* in its updated version, have gone to Adopt-A-Minefield, a programme connected with the United Nations Association, working to clear minefields and to provide assistance for survivors of landmine accidents. In putting the full focus of her charitable efforts into Adopt-A-Minefield, Heather brought back into the public spotlight the topic dear to Princess Diana's heart and a cause that Heather believed had been somewhat neglected in the years since Diana's death. At venues during recent tours Paul has worn a NO MORE LAND MINES! T-shirt on stage and put Adopt-A-Minefield products on sale along with his own McCartney merchandise not only at show venues but also via his website, www.paulmccartney.com.

Sir Paul had played some 58 concert dates for one million fans in 2002. The first concert date in Paul's diary for the following year brought his

Driving USA/ Back In The USA stage show across the Atlantic under a new title for the new year - *Back In The World*.

He began a European leg of his marathon world trek in Paris on March 25th, where he played for a capacity crowd at the Paris-Bercy Palais Omnisports Stadium. The band, mostly brought together for the *Driving Rain* studio sessions in America with producer David Kahne, consisted of keyboard player Paul 'Wix' Wickens, who has worked with Paul for many years now, guitarists Rusty Anderson and Brian Ray and drummer Abe Laboriel Jr.

The following month the tour came to Britain, England to be precise, four gigs in London, Birmingham, Manchester and, finally, Liverpool. The UK dates were interrupted in May for a history-making gig in Moscow's Red Square in the shadow of Lenin's tomb, Paul's first concert in the city. This might have been a Paul McCartney concert in just about any region of the planet, the audience holding their banners saying Paul We Love You Forever. They sang along with the lyrics of not only the golden oldies but also a few of the latest album tracks.

During their visit Paul and Heather met President Putin — who had attended the show — at the Kremlin, where Paul spoke of the unifying influence of music, and described The Beatles as a phenomenon of freedom. And as the television cameras recorded this extraordinary meeting of two mighty powers, Heather spoke about the ongoing need to clear the world of minefields once and forever.

Paul finished his latest series of stage shows at the beginning of June in Liverpool where some 30,000 fans gathered for his appearance at the specially constructed King's Dock Arena on the River Mersey's waterfront. Treated as his personal VIP guests, several hundred friends and members of the extended McCartney family clan attended. Paul said, "Halfway across the United States last year, I realised I must take this show back to Liverpool. This is the big one. This is the most emotional gig of the tour. Tonight I'm bringing it back home."

Another of the live highlights of Paul's year came on September 23rd, 2003, when the latest of his annual shows for the charity Adopt-A-Minefield took place in Los Angeles. At this year's event Paul was joined by special guest James Taylor. The last time the pair had been on stage together was almost exactly three years previously, when Taylor was inducted into the Rock & Roll Hall Of Fame. It was McCartney who gave him the honour. "We were just lucky to run into him," he said on handing over the Award. "He was just lucky to run into us, I suppose. And he started singing and it was just so beautiful, there and then we said, OK, he's on Apple.' So he was one of our very first artists on Apple."

Prior to the fund-raising event, Paul and Heather had told the charity's supporters, "The momentum we've seen in such a short time to rid the world of these insidious weapons of war has been extraordinary as well as gratifying. Adopt-A-Minefield has become a model for how people can work together to educate and make a difference. Each year, support for AAM grows and, more importantly, awareness of this world-wide crisis grows. Out of this growth we hope to eliminate a tragic, man-made epidemic." Paul did a set of 10 songs at the event and US talk-show presenter Jay Leno hosted the charity auction, which helped to swell total funds raised to 1.2 million dollars

Sir Paul McCartney: "It's what I do. You don't work music, you play music and I hope to be singing and playing when I'm 90 years old. I always thought I would live until about 90 and that estimate is going up! In the end I will probably be wheeled up on stage to sing 'Yesterday'."

ACKNOWLEDGMENTS

The creators of this book would like to thank the following for their inspiration, help, patience and support:

Andy Ewan, Vicky Holmes, Jim Newberry, Jerry Odlin, Lisa Ray, Lorna Russell, Virginia Lohle, Richard Kolnsberg, Bill May and Gerald Redila at Star File, and Richard Woolley.

Special thanks go to:

Corinne Barrow, for additional research
Debbie Lincoln, for editorial co-ordination
Susan Searle, for design management

And extra special thanks go to:

John, Paul, George and Ringo.

IMAGES

P1 Heather Mills McCartney & Sir Paul McCartney attending the 3rd Annual Adopt-A-Minefield Benefit Gala in Beverly Hills, September 2003. (Star File)

P2, 7, 22 Paul McCartney, Harry Goodwin (Star File)

P8 Robin Bextor & Sir Paul McCartney, Sussex, 2001 (RB Collection)

P10 Tony Barrow & The Beatles (TB Collection)

P12, 14, 17 Paul & Stella McCartney, Rock & Roll Hall Of Fame induction, Waldorf Astoria, New York, 2000 (RB Collection)

P19 Sir Paul McCartney, Sussex, 2001 (RB Collection)

P21 Woolton church, Woolton church fete programme, the McCartney family's house in Forthlin Road, Liverpool (RB Collection)

P25 The Beatles, Star Club, Hamburg, 1962, Danny Wall (Star File)

P27 Paul McCartney, painting by Klaus Voorman (RB Collection)

P28, 29 The Beatles, London 1964, Max Scheler (Star File)

P30,31 Montage: TSW TV special; the Cavern, Liverpool (TSW Archive, RB Collection)

P32 The Beatles meet the media in the USA (Star File)

P33 The Beatles on location for the filming of *Help!* (RB Collection)

P35 Paul McCartney's London (RB Collection)

P38, 39 Paul McCartney, Jane Asher and friends at Rishikesh (RB Collection)

P39 The Beatles promoting *Sgt Pepper's Lonely Hearts Club Band* in the summer of 1967 at the Apple Corps Offices in Savile Row, London (Star File)

P43 Paul McCartney, London, summer 1967 (Star File)

P46 The Beatles promoting *Sgt Pepper's Lonely Hearts Club Band* in the summer of 1967 at the Apple Corps Offices in Savile Row, London (Star File)

P47 McCartney, Laurens van Houten (Star File)

P49 The Beatles by Harry Goodwin (Star File)

P51 The Beatles in the Bahamas during the filming of *Help!* in 1965 (Star File)

P52 Then & Now montage (RB Collection)

P54 Sheila Johnston (RB Collection)

P56 Pete Best (RB Collection)

P58, 59 Paul McCartney at LIPA, 1994 (Jim Newberry)

P60 Voorman, and Hamburg nightlife (RB Collection)

P61 Klaus Voorman's painting of The Beatles (detail) (RB Collection)

P62 Bob Wooller (RB Collection)

P63 Paul McCartney & Wings (Star File)

P64 Bill Harry (RB Collection)

P65 Roger McGuinn (RB Collection)

P66 Peter Asher (RB Collection)

P68 Donovan (RB Collection)

P70, 71 Donovan & George Harrison at Rishikesh (RB Collection)

P72 Brian Wilson (RB Collection)

P73 Brian Wilson of The Beach Boys, 1966, Harry Goodwin (Star File)

P74 Michael Lindsay-Hogg (RB Collection)

P76 Neil Innes (RB Collection)

P78 Steve Miller (RB Collection)

P80 Steve Holly (RB Collection)

P81 Wings, Gered Mankowitz (Star File)

P82 Sir George Martin (RB Collection)

P84 The Beatles, Ivan Keenan (Star File)

P85 Paul and George (TSW Archive)

P86, 88 Paul McCartney (TSW Archive)

P90, 91 Paul McCartney, Astrid Kirchherr (Star File)

P92 Paul McCartney (TSW Archive)

P95 Front cover of *Meet The Beatles* featuring The Beatles, with Tony Barrow

P96 The Beatles (TSW Archive)

P98, 99 The Beatles face the press (Star File)

P100, 101 Paul McCartney reacts to press reports about himself (TSW Archive).

P103 Paul and Ringo off duty (TSW Archive)

P104 Paul acts up for the press (TSW Archive)

P106 Paul and John on stage, Jurgen Vollmer (Star File)

P109 Paul and Jane Asher in Rishikesh (RB Collection)

P111 P

P114 [ ] (e)

P115 [ ] gen Vollmer (Star File)

P117 [ ] Collection)

P119 [ ] Maharishi in Bangor (RB Collection)

P120 [ ] ction)

P12 [ ] File)

P12 [ ])

P126 Paul McCartney, Rock & Roll Hall Of Fame , Bob Gruen (Star File)

P130 Heather Mills and Paul McCartney after McCartney's concert for New York, 2001 (Star File)

P133–135, 140, 141 Driving USA tour, Michael Brito (Star File)